MAXIMIZING THE IMPACT OF C⟲ACHING CYCLES

GENE TAVERNETTI

JOHN CATT
FROM HODDER EDUCATION

Every effort has been made to trace all copyright holders, but if any have been inadvertently overlooked, the Publishers will be pleased to make the necessary arrangements at the first opportunity.

Although every effort has been made to ensure that website addresses are correct at time of going to press, Hodder Education cannot be held responsible for the content of any website mentioned in this book. It is sometimes possible to find a relocated web page by typing in the address of the home page for a website in the URL window of your browser.

Hachette UK's policy is to use papers that are natural, renewable and recyclable products and made from wood grown in well-managed forests and other controlled sources. The logging and manufacturing processes are expected to conform to the environmental regulations of the country of origin.

Orders: please contact Hachette UK Distribution, Hely Hutchinson Centre, Milton Road, Didcot, Oxfordshire, OX11 7HH. Telephone: +44 (0)1235 827827. Email education@hachette.co.uk. Lines are open from 9 a.m. to 5 p.m., Monday to Friday.

ISBN: 9781915261755

© Gene Tavernetti 2023

Illustrations by Carl Twisselman

First published in 2023 by
John Catt from Hodder Education,
An Hachette UK Company
15 Riduna Park, Station Road,
Melton, Woodbridge IP12 1QT
Telephone: +44 (0) 1394 389850

4500 140th Ave North,
Suite 101, Clearwater,
FL 33762-3848, US
Telephone: +1 561 448 1987

www.johncatt.com

A catalogue record for this title is available from the British Library

MIX
Paper | Supporting
responsible forestry
FSC™ C104740
FSC
www.fsc.org

In *Maximizing the Impact of Coaching Cycles*, coaching expert Gene Tavernetti provides an exceptionally clear, practical and humane guide to instructional coaching – informed by years of successful experience. Tavernetti also provides a frank and much-needed appraisal of the current dismal state of coaching. I learned vital lessons from reading this book and highly recommend it for coaches or any educator interested in improved teaching and learning.

Mike Schmoker, Author of FOCUS and Results Now 2.0

*Maximizing the Impact of Coaching Cycle*s is a rare gem in the crowded field of instructional leadership books. Tavernetti provides us with a practical, no-nonsense roadmap for implementing instructional coaching cycles, based on his extensive on-the-ground experience and expertise. Crucially, this book challenges instructional coaches to reclaim the core purpose of their work: supporting and developing teachers to improve student learning. This book is essential reading for anyone passionate about fostering excellence in instructional coaching, and it will undoubtedly become a well-worn resource on your professional bookshelf.

Dr. Zach Groshell Instructional Coach,
and Host of the Progressively Incorrect Podcast

It is rare to see professional development that is designed around the key concepts of a PLC where teachers are truly engaged in 'Learning by Doing.' Dr. Tavernetti's model of Coaching Cycles is an example of professional development in its most effective form. New and veteran teachers alike can access personal growth and continuous learning by participating. For me, as a district support provider, it was similarly simple to learn, to replicate, and to sustain from site to site and year to year. My district benefited greatly from his framework, and I can see it's effects year after year in the classroom with teachers.

George Knights, Director of Professional Learning Communities and
Assessment, Newport-Mesa Unified School District

If you are a principal who is lucky enough to have an instructional coach at your site, buy 2 copies of *Maximizing the Impact of Coaching Cycles* – one for you and one for your coach. This book tells you how to overcome the most common issues that prevent coaches from working with and being effective with all your teachers.

I know what Gene writes in this book works because for the past 20 years I have worked side by side with Dr. Tavernetti with dozens of my teachers in coaching cycles utilizing the strategies described in this book. All administrators and coaches who want to help teachers improve should keep a copy handy for reference.

James Hardin, Principal.

The common thread that weaves throughout everything that I've learned about coaching from Gene is that the key to successfully supporting others is ensuring that you build and sustain positive relationships. It's not about 'fixing' people. It's about acknowledging where they are and helping them envision where they can go from there.

Paul Dietrich, Academic Coach.

Reading this book was like watching a video of my coaching experience with Gene. Every step and element of the process and his detailed explanations are spot on. The introduction and implementation of the Teach FAST framework and Coaching Cycles are the most important responsibilities that should be undertaken by every site administrator! Even if a site administrator does not have access to an instructional coach, this book will educate and inspire! To teach at the very highest level, every teacher needs a coach!

Ken Valburg, Principal (Retired)

In my over 30 years in education, I have never experienced a coaching model as powerful, deep, and easy as the one Gene Tavernetti's book describes. This coaching model is rooted in a conceptual framework of collaborative and multi-faceted professional participation and engagement and results in improved learning for students, improved instruction for teachers, improved instructional leadership for administrators, and most importantly a common language for all professionals involved.

This is not a one-shot coaching miracle. It is a practice that is transformative of the educational professional learning community because it is applied to all learning situations over time. Even if you think, 'How can we possibly apply the coaching framework to THIS learning situation?' You can, and your whole team will grow professionally by engaging and reflecting on the art and science of teaching through this coaching framework. So, enjoy the coaching ride. I can assure you won't want to get off when you see how the light bulbs turn on as your students 'get it'!

Carin Contreras, Assistant Superintendent of Instruction

CONTENTS

PREFACE

If you were to read a selection of job descriptions for instructional coaches, you would find a laundry list of activities that each coach would be expected to perform once employed. They would include such things as:

- Arranging professional development activities for all teachers in the school.
- Staying on top of changes in state standards and assessments and communicating these to teachers.
- Building strong relationships with teachers and administrators.
- Researching new resources and evidence-based strategies for instruction, assessment, classroom management, and student engagement.
- Testing and promoting the latest tools and technologies for teaching.
- Supporting teachers in using student-level data to improve instruction.
- Assisting teachers with developing differentiated lessons, planning and pacing lessons, and implementing best practices to meet the needs of students.
- Informally observing lessons and providing feedback for teacher growth.
- Assisting with the development of systems and structures to improve schoolwide teacher practice and student engagement.
- Attending professional development seminars and workshops for instructional coaches.

An instructional coach could work all day, every day, performing most of the duties listed here and have no face-to-face interactions with teachers.

Hidden amongst the activities that require minimal or no face-to-face coaching with teachers is 'Assisting teachers with developing differentiated lessons, planning and pacing lessons, and implementing best practices to meet the needs of students.' This book is devoted to that 'hidden' job of planning, observing, and providing feedback to teachers, i.e. coaching cycles. Coaching cycles are the most impactful contacts an instructional coach can have with a teacher.

Often you will read a blurb on a book jacket cover that boldly states, 'This is the last book you will ever need on instructional coaching!' If this is the last book you read about instructional coaching that would be fine. If this is the first book you read about instructional coaching that would also be fine. Just don't make this the only book you ever read about instructional coaching.

Maximizing the Impact of Coaching Cycles addresses issues, roadblocks, and fears faced by coaches, coaches of coaches, and administrators in effectively launching and facilitating a program of coaching.

Like my previous book, *Teach FAST* (2022), this is not a textbook citing all the most germane research. And like my previous book, the advice is based on my experiences in doing the work, coaching teachers and administrators, and operationalizing findings from research. If you are familiar with the research on coaching, you will recognize it embedded in these tips and suggestions. That said, all the strategies presented here are based on nearly 20 years of coaching experiences in the field. They are not the theoretical musings of an ivory tower brain trust. I have personally faced all the issues discussed in this book. My approach is research grounded but has also been thoroughly field-tested and found to be helpful and successful.

If you are a coach, a coach of coaches, or an administrator, following these suggestions will help you achieve a much larger return on your coaching investment. There will be more teachers coached, increased instructional effectiveness, and ultimately increased student achievement.

PART ONE
INTRODUCTION

RATIONALE FOR THE BOOK

Imagine you have no experience with the guitar, and you decide to take lessons. You can't wait to learn some of your favorite songs. You arrive for your first lesson but as you begin to open your guitar case, your instructor tells you to just leave it closed.

The teacher sits down and gives you a history of the guitar. Using his guitar, he teaches you the names of the guitar parts. He then shows you a video that repeats much of the information. The lesson is almost over. Before you leave, he gives you a quiz on the names of the parts of the guitar. After the quiz, your teacher praises you for how well you did on your first guitar lesson. Next week, he says, you will learn the names for all the strings.

Finally, he says, 'You won't need your guitar next week either; I'll let you know when you need it. There is a so much to learn about guitars.'

Frustrated, you proclaim, 'All wanted to do was learn the three chords to play *Louie Louie*'.

Several years ago, a school district I later worked with selected approximately 50 teachers from each of their high and middle schools to serve as instructional coaches.[1] After a year of training by an independent consultant, the district administration and the coaches became disenchanted with the current consultants and the training that had been provided. After a year of extensive training not a single coach had met

---

1   The term instructional coaches will be used throughout this book as an all-inclusive term that includes instructional coaches, academic coaches, content area coaches, literacy coaches, edtech coaches, etc.

with a single teacher to discuss instruction.

In one sense it was good that the coaches did not meet with teachers. After a year of training, the coaches were still not prepared to meet one-on-one with teachers to facilitate a coaching cycle; the most impactful framework for coach-teacher interactions.

In my conversations with the district administrators, I learned that the coaches had found the content of the training to be 'Important, interesting, and insightful'. The prospective coaches had learned about different types of instructional coaching and various roles they might assume as an instructional coach. They learned the difference between coaches and consultants, counselors, or mentors. They learned about the critical role trust played in coaching relationships. They learned about the importance of developing rapport with the teachers they would be coaching.

Coaches do need to develop rapport with teachers. Teachers need to trust coaches. Coaches also need to respect teachers. However, what was missing from the curriculum was how this respect, rapport, and trust manifest and are utilized during the most crucial and impactful coaching activity, one-on-one coaching during a coaching cycle.

It is as if the trainers had told the coaches, 'You need to respect the teachers, develop rapport with the teachers, develop trust with the teachers and yada, yada, yada go do coaching cycles.'[2]

Shortly after agreeing to assume the training of these coaches, I spoke with several of them about their training. After a year, none of the coaches felt prepared. They all had specific questions about how to work one-on-one with a teacher:

- How do I initiate conversations with teachers about instruction?
- How do I coach veteran teachers who are more experienced than I am?
- How do I start a reflection conversation with a teacher after a lesson that didn't go well?
- What if teachers are rude and mean?

---

2   Seinfeld S8.E19.

- What do I say to teachers who think I went to 'the dark side'?[3]

These new coaches, many driven by fear, were asking the right questions.

In another district where I had also been hired to train coaches around the same time, they came *tabula rasa*, with no prior training. This group of coaches also had questions:

- How do I initiate conversations with teachers about instruction?
- How do I coach veteran teachers who are more experienced than I am?
- How do I start a reflection conversation with a teacher after a lesson that didn't go well?
- What if teachers are rude and mean?
- What do I say to teachers who think I went to the 'dark side'?

These new coaches, many driven by fear, were also asking the right questions.

I gave both groups of coaches, the one with extensive previous training in theory and the other without, the same material. My training focused on how to effectively facilitate coaching cycles. All the coaches' questions were answered in the context of the most impactful work, the most difficult work: working one-on-one with teachers in their classrooms to improve instruction. In other words, my training focused on the information they most needed to know.

The purpose of this book is to fill the gaps that many resources omit. This missing information is exactly what principals and coaches need to know to launch, or relaunch, a successful coaching program.

This book is organized into four parts.

Part One: Introducing Coaching Cycles, provides a brief description of coaching cycles, their benefits, and why they are integral to a school's system of instructional improvement.

Part Two: Before Coaching Begins, addresses what administrators and coaches need to know and do in order to launch and maintain an effective

---

3   The dark side is a term used by some teachers to describe administration.

coaching program. If you have already begun a coaching program, it is never too late relaunch it more effectively. The information found in this book is evergreen.

Part Three: Coaching Cycles, is an in-depth how-to manual for maximizing the impact the impact of coaching cycles. Many of the questions the new coaches above asked are answered here.

Part Four: Miscellaneous Tips and Getting Started, the dos and don'ts that any new coach should be aware of without having to learn them the hard way, and some final words of wisdom and encouragement.

COACHING CYCLES

Big Ideas:

- One-on-one (Personalized PD).
- What is a coaching cycle?
- Benefits of coaching cycles.
- Why coaching cycles are not used more.

Overview

There are many activities in any coach's job description. It is common for instructional coaches to support teachers by leading PD, training teachers in administrative procedures (such as a new on-line grading system), sharing research, and the infamous 'other duties as assigned.' However, the activity which has by far the most impact on improving instruction is meeting one-on-one with teachers to facilitate coaching cycles.

Coaching cycles provide an opportunity for coaches to peek into the instructional practices and thoughts of the teachers they are working with. This information provides the coach with a roadmap to support individual teachers as well as the wider staff of a given institution.

ONE-ON-ONE COACHING

For more than a century, educators have chosen sides in the ongoing saga of 'Edu Wars' between progressive or traditional approaches. However, there is near universal agreement across this divide that the most effective and impactful support a person can receive is personalized, one-on-one coaching. This method has been successfully used for centuries by skilled craftsmen in apprenticeship programs. Master craftsmen, working one-on-one with a novice, were able to provide personalized, just-in-time feedback and reflection on the novice's performance. Coaching cycles provide similar individualized support to meet the needs of all teachers from novices to experts.

Agreement about the impact of one-on-one support is not only common sense but also reflected in most current academic literature and popular media. The most impactful support comes through collaboratively planning a lesson, observing the teacher teach that lesson, and then meeting for just-in-time feedback and reflection about the lesson. Although you may encounter various names for this type of support, I use the term 'coaching cycle'.[4]

Like any activity, there are effective ways for coaches to facilitate coaching cycles and ways that are a waste of time. This book is focused on how coaches can be effective and efficient when working with teachers during the coaching cycles.

WHAT IS A COACHING CYCLE?

A coaching cycle consists of a sequence of activities, usually conducted over two to three days:

- Pre-observation: the teacher and coach meet to collaboratively discuss and plan a lesson which the teacher will then present.
- Observation: the teacher presents the lesson, the coach observes.
- Post-observation: the teacher and coach meet to reflect and debrief the lesson.

PRE-OBSERVATION

The goal of the pre-observation is for the teacher and the coach to thoroughly discuss a lesson that the teacher will then present. The coach's role is to facilitate this discussion by asking the teacher questions about the lesson. The coach's questions serve as a model for the type of questions that teachers should be asking themselves when designing a lesson, or

---

4   Hattie, J. (2008) *Visible Learning: A synthesis of over 800 meta-analyses relating to achievement.* New York: Routledge; Hattie, J. (2011) *Visible Learning for Teachers: Maximizing impact on learning.* New York: Routledge; Knight, J. (2019) *The Impact Cycle: What instructional coaches should to foster powerful improvements.* Thousand Oaks, CA: Corwin.

using a lesson designed by someone else, to ensure that the instructional focus has been met. Without a mutually agreed instructional focus – an alignment about what is good – it is extremely difficult for the teacher and coach to have a meeting of minds.

The questions that a coach asks are not meant to be a test for the teacher. Rather these questions are posed to help guide collaboration. By asking questions, and then working through answers collaboratively, the coach models how to effectively collaborate with colleagues to design lessons.

OBSERVATION

The coach observes the lesson that was collaboratively planned. This should be a real lesson, in a real classroom with the teacher's regular students. In that environment, the coach can collect valid and reliable data on the teacher's ability to deliver a well-designed lesson.

POST-OBSERVATION

This is the opportunity for the teacher to reflect and debrief the lesson with the coach. The teacher can describe and self-evaluate the pluses and minuses of the lesson design and delivery as related to goals set forth during the pre-observation planning.

BENEFITS OF COACHING CYCLES

INDIVIDUAL FORMATIVE ASSESSMENT

Coaching cycles give the coach the opportunity to observe a teacher in three phases critical to instruction. They provide real-time formative data on a teacher's ability to plan, teach, and reflect on lessons. Each of the three parts of the lesson cycle are distinct yet interconnected parts of the instructional process.

Most teacher preparation programs provide pre-service *education* about planning and teaching lessons, but many of these programs lack pre-service *training*. Based on teachers' articulate explanations following this kind of education one would expect near perfect lesson execution. In reality, the result of this type of preparation often produces new teachers who can talk intelligently and fluently *about* planning and teaching lessons but cannot actually plan and teach effectively.

One of my first contracts was with an entity that was being sued by the Office of Civil Rights. The entity had been investigated and found to be providing inadequate language acquisition instruction to students who were English learners. Our job was to assess the teaching staff's current knowledge and instructional practices, and then provide training to ensure all students were receiving quality instruction.

We interviewed every teacher to determine their current knowledge regarding best practices for the instruction of English learners. We also observed every teacher to evaluate their current instructional practices. During our teacher interviews we found that nearly 100% of the teachers were able to articulate the most effective teaching strategies. During our observation we found that very few of those same teachers were employing those strategies. The teachers had been educated but not trained.

Working one-on-one with a teacher during a coaching cycle provides the most complete and coherent picture of a teacher's instructional expertise. The three phases force a teacher to talk the talk and walk the walk.

One of the first truths a new instructional coach discovers is that what transpires in the classroom often does not match what is being described in the staff room. Teachers who were always thought to be effective based on conversations, can be found to be dismal in the classroom. This is an especially difficult realization when a coach's first assignment is at a school where they have previously taught. Folks can hide in a classroom when their door is closed. They can't hide during a coaching cycle.

SCHOOLWIDE DATA

Having *all* teachers at a school participate in coaching cycles provides formative data that can be generalized to identify and prioritize areas of need across the entire school. This data will inform the coach and administration about the support and professional development needs of the entire staff. Determining staff development needs from data drawn from the entire staff is respectful to everyone. If a principal does not direct *all* staff to participate in a coaching cycle, then that principal will miss the opportunity to gain a schoolwide understanding of their staff's development needs.

WHY COACHING CYCLES ARE NOT USED MORE

There are many ways in which coaches can support teachers. Most of these activities require minimal interpersonal contact between the coach and teacher: finding curriculum resources, sharing research, doing demonstration lessons, giving professional development presentations, etc. These tasks often fall within the scope of the job description and performing them allows a coach to feel busy. But these tasks lack the impact of coaching cycles. It is the perfect illustration of Pareto's 80/20 principle: 80% of the impact coaches have, can come from 20% of their time (i.e. facilitating coaching cycles). Instead of focusing on the most important activity that can impact instruction, the coach is 'busy' performing other tasks the school deems to be urgent. This is not always the fault of the coach.

When a school experiences low achievement, every aspect of the instructional program is examined. However, the last thing that is usually addressed is instructional effectiveness. Instead, the instructional coach is deployed to support all the other variables that may impact student achievement.

One of the first things a school will look at when experiencing low achievement is the curriculum. If students are not doing well, it must be because they don't have the proper materials. Coaches and other personnel are used to pilot a new curriculum and then help to train other teachers in it. It may take years for a school to select and implement a new curriculum. During the time it takes to implement the new curriculum, judgements and measurements of achievement levels are granted a grace period. Afterall, how can anyone be held accountable while they are learning how to use something new?

But what happens when the new curriculum is in place, the grace period is over, and students are still not achieving? The problem must be the lack of an intervention program. Entire systems are created for identifying and placing students into a new intervention program. Positions are created. Teacher assignments are changed. Schedules are changed. Coaches are utilized to provide training in the new intervention programs.

After a time, when the intervention program is judged not to be working as well as originally hoped, it is determined that students have not been properly placed in the interventions. Committees meet. Teachers attend workshops. New assessments and rubrics are created. Staff receive training in how to administer the new assessments. IT gets involved and new databases are created, the school's dashboard is updated. Teachers need additional training in the new databases and the new dashboard. The coaches are called upon to provide that training.

In some schools the most effective teachers are assigned to teach the lowest achieving students in the intervention program. Not surprisingly, the students begin to perform better. It is difficult to attribute the cause of the progress because the impact of the intervention program, and new assessments, are confounded by the students receiving more effective instruction.

Students are placed in intervention classes using a different assessment and they still do not achieve. Maybe they need a different intervention curriculum. And on and on it goes.

I remember walking into a sporting goods store that sold used golf clubs. There was a sign on the door that read, 'You don't need $1,000 golf clubs if you have a $150 swing.' The message of course was to begin with the basics.

For many golfers the answer to poor scores is to buy new clubs. For most schools the answer to poor scores is to buy a new curriculum, a new program, or a new technology. In both instances the first step should be to work with a coach to make sure you are the best you can be with your current resources. Coaching cycles get teachers to a shared baseline of knowledge, a shared baseline of competency. Coaching cycles impact instruction to make effective instruction a constant, not a variable, when looking at solutions for improved student achievement.

Coaching cycles may be the most impactful activity in which a coach can participate, but they are also the activity that requires the highest level of skill. The reason why coaching cycles are not the first thing a school does is that they are the hardest work. They are hard because they involve working one-on-one, face-to-face with teachers. All of the other activities mentioned above in efforts to improve student performance – developing a curriculum, assessment, schedules, and so on – involve working on things and can be performed with minimal feedback to teachers themselves. Things don't push back, things don't complain, things don't have egos that need to be managed, but people do.

Many coaches with whom I have worked expressed more than a touch of trepidation about engaging teachers in coaching cycles. They had many questions about how to navigate challenges both real and imagined. For example, they asked how to coach a teacher who is more experienced, how to coach a teacher who teaches content outside of their area of expertise, what to do if a teacher is resistant or non-cooperative. These concerns, and others, are common, real, and are addressed in this book.

ROADMAP TO TEACHER AUTONOMY

Big Ideas:

- Goal of instructional coaching.
- Roadmap to teacher autonomy.
- Coaching cycles are part of the improvement system.
- Gradual release in coaching cycles.

GOALS OF INSTRUCTIONAL COACHING

Having a coaching program is a means to an end, it is not the goal in itself. Developing a program that complements other elements of the school's system of improvement is the goal. The common goals of all systems of instructional improvement are instructional efficacy in the classroom, and teacher autonomy, i.e. the ability of teachers to collaboratively examine data and decide on next actions.

To achieve these goals the entire school staff needs to be trained and led to these outcomes. This is not meant to disrespect the knowledge or expertise of teachers. In fact, every word in this book should be interpreted to show and demonstrate the highest respect for teachers. Administrators and coaches need to give respect to teachers, but not total deference.

ROADMAP TO TEACHER AUTONOMY

The roadmap to teacher autonomy and collaboration includes several stops: Training, one-on-one coaching cycles, teacher-partner coaching cycles, and lesson studies. The 'lesson study' is another one of those terms in education that is in common usage without a common definition. I use the term to describe a process in which a group of teachers collaboratively plan a lesson, then consecutively teach that lesson while being observed by their partners, and finally provide feedback to each other to perfect the lesson.

TRAINING

All teachers need common training before coaching cycles begin to provide a shared understanding about the school's area of focus, and a common vocabulary, with common definitions that will allow subsequent discussion and collaboration.

There are many words that we use in education that we assume to be understood and agreed upon by all, but this may not be the case. A partial list of such words includes: mini-lesson, activity, guided practice, gradual release, discovery, etc.

I recall one long Saturday in a doctoral level course discussing and attempting to agree upon the meaning of 'curriculum'. After what seemed like hours of debate and discussion there was still no agreement.

Training that provides a teaching staff with a common understanding of the terms, areas of focus, and other miscellaneous bits will prevent wasted time during subsequent coaching cycles.

ONE-ON-ONE COACHING CYCLES

If the entire process of bringing coaching cycles to a staff were thought of as a lesson, the initial training would provide the explanation of concepts and modeling. One-on-one coaching during coaching cycles is the beginning of practice, or more specifically guided practice; the initial repetition of practice where teachers apply information presented during the training. It is also the beginning of the process of gradual release of responsibility by the coach to teacher.

Depending on the teacher, one or two one-on-one coaching cycles will be sufficient for them to confidently continue without direct support from the coach.

COACHING CYCLE WITH PARTNER

Continuing the analogy of the roadmap being like a lesson, the next step of the coaching cycle – which pairs two teachers – is a further release of responsibility from the coach to the teachers. Both teacher-partners will themselves have completed one or two individual coaching cycles before this collaboration. They will share a common terminology and understanding of the process.

Think of this step as an intermediate stop on the road to teachers leading coaching cycles themselves (i.e. autonomously). The coach should plan on facilitating one or two of these sessions, providing opportunities for each teacher to lead during the planning process. The coach serves as a facilitator as needed.

LESSON STUDY

I am defining a 'lesson study' as the collaboration of a group of two or more teachers to design a lesson, consecutively teach and observe each member of the group teach the lesson, and then collaboratively reflect on the design and delivery of the lesson. The purpose of a lesson study is to provide teachers with practice autonomously using data to identify areas of weakness in the curriculum, and then designing more successful alternatives at the classroom level.

A lesson study is the ultimate goal of a coaching cycle. If a coaching cycle with a partner is guided practice, then a lesson study – teachers working with a larger team – is independent practice. Because all the participating teachers have been through both one-on-one coaching cycles, and coaching cycles with a partner, these teachers need less and less facilitative support in the process from the coach. When teachers reach this point of the journey, the coach's role further evolves from facilitator to observer.

DON'T SKIP STEPS

Collaborating without shared knowledge is not possible. A shared baseline of common knowledge and experience makes participation by every teacher possible. If one or more teachers are perceived to have knowledge others lack, some teachers may mistakenly defer to them.

FREQUENTLY ASKED QUESTIONS

Question: When teachers begin to perform coaching cycles with a colleague, how much should I intervene?

Answer: As much as necessary, but no more. Think of this stage of development as guided practice during a lesson. If the students are successful, no intervention is necessary. If the students need assistance, start with a nudge, a hint. Intervene as little as possible. Only by observing the teachers engage in the work can you collect the formative data you need to prescribe the proper support.

Question: If I follow this roadmap and teachers will be able to collaboratively plan, observe, and provide feedback. Am I working myself out of a job?

Answer: No. There may be fewer teachers who will need initial exposure to coaching cycles, but there will always be new teachers who will need you to coach them through coaching cycles. There will always be something you can do to support teachers to help them get better.

PART TWO
BEFORE COACHING CYCLES BEGIN

ADMINISTRATION: ESTABLISHING A BASELINE

Big Ideas:

- Identify areas of improvement.
- Agreement on instructional strategies.
- Establishing a baseline.

OVERVIEW

The principal bears ultimate responsibility for the quality of instruction in their school. Prior to the ubiquity of instructional coaches, the principal had sole responsibility for observing teachers, diagnosing teachers, and supporting their improvement. While principals are still ultimately responsible, instructional coaches now shoulder much of that day-to-day work.

The job of the coach is to help teachers get better, to become more effective. Before a coach can begin this work there must be an explicit agreement about what effective instruction looks like that is shared by the coach, principal, and staff. Without this shared understanding, any suggestions a coach may provide a teacher to improve their instruction can be easily reduced to a mere opinion. A teacher may respond to a suggestion by saying, 'That isn't how I do it. I like my way.' Without such an agreement, every opinion about quality instruction is equally valid. When every opinion is equally valid, the coach's impact on improvement becomes dramatically impaired.

IDENTIFY AREAS OF IMPROVEMENT

It is the responsibility of the principal to lead a process that brings the staff to a consensus on what should be seen in all classrooms, i.e. effective instructional strategies to be used by every teacher. There are many techniques a principal may employ to reach such a consensus that are outside the scope of this book. But bringing a staff to agreement on strategies that should be employed in every classroom is too important a task to be left to chance or someone with limited experience of leading group processes. It is the responsibility of the principal to ensure the process occurs, but if she lacks the experience, she does not have to lead the process personally.

Ideally, the actions suggested in this chapter would have occurred before your coaching program began. If you have already begun your coaching program without having done these things, and it is not going as well as you would like, it is not too late to do them now.

The instructional areas of focus that are ultimately agreed upon by the staff should be non-controversial and evergreen. *Non-controversial* areas of focus are approaches that all staff members agree are beneficial for student learning. Non-controversial instructional strategies that should be utilized in every classroom include such things as effective checking for understanding, using student feedback to adjust lessons, maximizing student engagement, just to name a few. These are difficult for any staff member to argue against. Notice that these non-controversial areas of focus simply identify 'what' should occur. Most of these areas of focus allow individual teachers to be somewhat flexible in 'how' they are achieved.

Evergreen means that the focus will survive regardless of the newest educational technology, latest curriculum, or current fad. You may have noticed that non-controversial instructional strategies, such as those listed above, will also qualify as evergreen.

In some districts there seems to be a new district initiative declared every year. Such initiatives are usually generated by a district committee that attended a conference together. The initiatives are usually very popular throughout their state and may also be popular in large sections of the country.

I have always wondered where these ideas are generated. Wherever they originate they are pervasive. It seems like every principal throughout the state will have a copy of the same latest educational book that has the answer to all the current problems in education.

The initiative (of the year) is usually announced at a big beginning of the year assembly where the entire district is in attendance. The new initiative will usually have a transition period during which all teachers must attend days and days of training.

In these days of 'initiative of the year thinking', is consensus possible on non-controversial and evergreen instructional strategies? In these times of 'Edu Wars' over traditional versus progressive approaches and all the peripheral topics around them, can staff reach agreement and coalesce around effective instructional initiatives?[5] My experience tells me the answer is yes. In fact, if a coaching program is to have an impact on instruction, this agreement must happen before coaching cycles can begin.

AGREEMENT ON INSTRUCTIONAL STRATEGIES

Like all professions, education has its own specialized vocabulary. There are many words used by educators that are so common that no one seems to question what they mean, or how a speaker is using them. However, it is only when both parties in a conversation share a common understanding about the use of a word that discussions about the concepts embedded in it can truly begin. Principals must ensure that everyone is on the same page when identifying areas of focus for instructional improvement.

Identified areas of focus, arrived at by consensus, provide teachers with common goals for instruction. It is one thing to agree that all teachers will check for understanding. It is quite another for everyone to agree on what *effective* checking for understanding looks like. The staff may have agreed on the words that name the strategies, but there may not be agreement on what it means to operationalize those strategies in the classroom.

---

5   When I am working with a school, I always argue for a model of instruction that will include all the areas of focus that I described in *Teach FAST* (2022).

Reaching this consensus must then be followed by a PD to establish a common understanding and vocabulary in staff around the school's areas of focus. A pre-requisite for such a PD is the principal and coach sharing an understanding of the areas of focus and exactly what they should look like in a classroom when implemented correctly (although in practice there will be some flexibility in how these areas of focus are achieved by each teacher).

Imagine that a principal and a coach are observing a teacher's lesson, and they hear the teacher ask her students, 'Does anyone have any questions? If there are no questions, I must assume that everyone understands.' If the principal and coach have not reached a consensus, then the principal may judge that the teacher successfully checked for understanding, while the coach might well correctly evaluate the teacher's checking for understanding as ineffective.

The principal and the coach must reach agreement about what constitutes effective employment of the areas of instructional focus. The demonstrable elements of that agreement must be provided to staff during an effective PD. Only in this way can a shared understanding about what is good, what is effective, be developed.

ESTABLISHING A BASELINE

The only valid and reliable way to make determinations about the effectiveness of instructional program interventions is to control as many variables as possible. How can a new curriculum be evaluated if poor instruction continues? Uniform application of non-controversial and evergreen strategies can help provide a more valid analysis of performance data.

FREQUENTLY ASKED QUESTIONS

Question: Where can I find non-controversial and evergreen instructional strategies?

Answer: My first recommendation is my own *Teach FAST* (2022). It is a coherent lesson framework that embeds many individual strategies that could be selected. Other recommendations include Tom Sherrington's

Rosenshine's Principles in Action (2019), Marzano's 9 instructional strategies, and Doug Lemov's *Teach Like a Champion* (2014).

Question: Do staff have to reach consensus on the areas of focus?

Answer: Yes. You will never get 100% agreement on everything. Consensus should be reached around what the areas of focus or expected outcomes should be. However, because teachers are a diverse group flexibility will be needed in how those areas of focus will be achieved. This can be individually decided by teachers in conjunction with the coach.

JUST TELL THEM

Big Ideas:

- The principal is responsible if teachers do not meet with the coach.
- Meeting with the coach is not optional.
- 'Why do I have to meet with a coach?'
- Confidence in the coach.

OVERVIEW

> There comes a point when we need to stop pulling people out of the river. We need to go upstream and find out why they are falling in.

Every book about coaching, every article or blog ever written, every video, webinar, or in-person training discusses problems that are nearly universal. The most common problem reported that prevents coaches from being more effective is the small percentage of teachers who volunteer to meet with coaches. Every book, article, blog, etc. provides tips and strategies for the coach to help increase the number of teachers who will choose to work the coach. Many tips suggest the coach providing treats such as doughnuts or chocolate at teacher meetings (who doesn't love doughnuts and chocolate?). All these resources neglect to address one important question. Who bears responsibility for teachers not meeting with the coach? As the old adage quoted above puts it, who is upstream throwing people into the river?

RESPONSIBILITY FOR TEACHERS NOT MEETING WITH THE COACH

School districts have invested significant resources to staff schools with coaches to support teachers. The districts view coaching as an integral part of the school's instructional improvement system. Does the principal view quality instruction optional?

If all teachers are not meeting with the coach, 100% of the blame should be attributed to the school's principal. Principals can increase the percentage of teachers working with the coach to 100% by clearly stating, 'All teachers are expected to meet with the coach for a coaching cycle.' This eliminates the issue of teachers choosing not to volunteer to meet with the coach. Meeting with the coach for a coaching cycle is not optional. If all teachers participate, then it will maximize the impact of coaches on the instructional improvement system.

Notice that all teachers are only expected to 'meet' with the coach. That language has been chosen very carefully. It is the responsibility of the principal to get the teacher and the coach together for a coaching cycle. After that it is the coach's responsibility to develop a *working* relationship with teachers. The administrator can lead teachers to the coach, but she can't make them drink the Kool-Aid.

Why wouldn't every principal require all teachers to meet with the coach? The two main reasons are:

1. The principal does not believe that the teacher and the school will benefit from every teacher meeting with the coach.
2. The principal lacks confidence in the coach.

EMOTIONAL BELIEF

If a principal does not believe that every teacher, and the school, will benefit from participating in a coaching cycle then she will not know how to respond when a teacher says, 'I have been teaching for 10 years. I am a good teacher. Why do I have to work with a coach?' Without belief in the benefits of coaching for all staff it would be easy for the principal to fold and acquiesce to an objecting teacher.

The principal must be able to express a policy statement, 'Everyone will meet with the coach.' Without belief in the benefits of coaching cycles to the instructional program, comments like those above will turn into a debate about this teacher or that teacher becoming exempt. When that happens, you might as well start counting the bodies drowning in the river.

The principal needs to believe in the benefits of coaching both intellectually and emotionally. Most principals know that coaching can be beneficial. There is a plethora of reports and evidence available on the positive impact of coaching on instruction. This intellectual belief will be maintained until challenged by new data.

The second type of belief is emotional belief. People who believe something emotionally have had some type of experience that cements this belief in a more permanent manner. Emotional belief creates strength, creates courage. Principals who know and believe in the impact of instructional coaching have no problem telling staff that everyone will meet with the coach. People often ask me if I am bothered by reluctant teachers. I reply, 'No, because I know how the story ends. When teachers decide to try new things, students learn more.'

In one district I worked in, every administrator was told by their district-level boss that they would receive the same training as their teachers in order to infuse emotional belief about the power of coaching in them. In addition to the training, every administrator went through the same coaching cycle as teachers. In other words, the principals and assistant principals also planned a lesson, were observed teaching, and received feedback. Every one of these principals and assistant-principals exited the experience with emotional belief about the coaching cycle. The emotions they expressed ranged from, 'I wish I'd known this when I was teaching', and 'This makes me want to teach again', to 'I didn't take it very seriously and was a little embarrassed. You called me out honestly and gently.'

At the end of the coaching cycle, every principal expressed emotional learning. At the very least, after experiencing the coaching cycle, a principal was able to say to a reluctant or resistant teacher, 'I felt the same way you do before I did it. Trust me, it will be okay.'

Here is another answer to the veteran teacher's question of 'why do I need to meet with the coach?'

> The coach is not meeting with every teacher to tell them what they are doing wrong. The reason all teachers are doing coaching cycles is for the coach to understand what all teachers are doing. Meeting with the coach will allow her to see all the good things going on in

your classroom. It is possible that after meeting with you, the coach will be sharing your successful strategies and techniques with other teachers. We are committed to the philosophy of the professional learning community, where we all learn from each other.

CONFIDENCE IN THE COACH

The second reason a principal may hesitate to simply tell the staff to meet with the coach is a lack of confidence in the coach. If the principal fears a constant line of teachers at her door to complain about the coach and tell her what a waste of time it was, it is easy for the administrator to backslide on what *every* teacher means. It won't seem worth the effort.

Ensuring that all staff members meet with the coach for a coaching cycle is the responsibility of the principal. Principals must have confidence in the ability of their coaches. If they do not have confidence in the coach, then they need a new coach, or to provide a coach for the coach.

The principal must ensure the coach is ready for the job. Coaches, especially new coaches, benefit greatly from having their own coach. There are many interactions new coaches will have with teachers that need to be processed with someone more experienced. There are many problems that the coach may handle but are not quite sure if they could have handled better.

An experienced coach can support a new coach in a variety of ways. One of the most important is how to impact the entire staff more quickly. There are instances where coaches simply do not know what is possible.

Very early in my career I worked in a school where the principal proudly informed me that the school's instructional improvement goal for the year was that every teacher would write the learning objective for their lesson on the white board. That was it. The goal for an entire year was to write a sentence on the board! Being new I just smiled and nodded. If that were to happen today, I would express how the principal was selling the staff short. The staff are capable of much more. The principal should ask for more. That perspective is what an experienced coach can provide.

How do you find a coach for your coach? There are several ways to find the right person. Below are three ideas and some cautions for each.

#1 The person who trained your coach

If your coach had prior training, ask them if they would be confident having that person act as their coach.

Caution: There are organizations that operate a 'trainer of trainers' model. This means that the trainer may be expert in delivering a training script but may not have requisite experience in difficult coaching circumstances. It is one thing to deliver a training script, and quite another to have the experience to navigate through difficult interactions.

#2 County Offices/Regional Offices Consortiums/State Offices of Education

Because nearly every district now employs instructional coaches, most county or regional programs provide some training for coaches. At an additional cost, these entities will also be happy to provide additional coaching.

Caution: Many people who work for county or regional office may not feel the urgency to ensure a coach and their teachers improve because their job will still exist regardless outcomes. Be sure that you can pick and contract an individual of your choosing rather than just working with the agency itself. In a large agency the person who is assigned to your coach may not be the same person who provided the training and is known to you.

#3 Private Professional Development Companies

There are several well-known national development companies that have a stable of consultants who are loosely tied to the company as independent contractors.

Caution: Like the country or regional programs, the person 'assigned' to your school may not be the same person who provided previous training, or the person known to you.

Finding a Coach for Your Coach

Ideas for finding the right person:

- The person who trained your coach
- County/regional offices
- Private professional development companies

One final caution: Do not let the fact that a company is a 'non-profit' sway your decision making. Some people assume that a non-profit means that costs will be less, or that the people working there have a bigger heart and make less money than in a for profit company. The reality is that the only real distinction between a non-profit and a for profit company as it relates to the client, is that the former has an income stream that may not be directly related to client outcomes such as support from grants or foundations.

I was once asked by an educator if my company was non-profit. I replied, 'No, we have to get results.'

FREQUENTLY ASKED QUESTIONS

Question: I have a veteran teacher who has very clearly expressed that she does not want to be coached. What do I tell her?

Answer: You smile, listen respectfully, and repeat your policy statement. 'Every teacher will meet with the coach for a coaching cycle.'

I continue to be surprised by this question. What do you tell a teacher who says she does not want to arrive to class on time? What do you tell a teacher who says she does not want to do attendance? What do you tell a teacher who does not want to give students grades?

Question: My coach is new. How do I get the confidence to turn her loose with tough staff?

Answer: Three suggestions. The first is to choose the initial cohort strategically. This will allow the coach to gain experience with 'friendlier' staff members (see 'Choosing the First Cohort for a Coaching Cycle'). The second is to hire a competent coach for your coach. Third, look for other opportunities for the new coach to shadow other existing coaches to increase their exposure to various teachers, lessons, and circumstances.

RELATIONSHIP BUILDING

Big Ideas:

- Establishing relationships.
- Mixer.
- Getting coffee.
- A good buzz.
- First date.

OVERVIEW

Impactful coaches develop positive relationships with the teachers they coach. These relationships are built on trust and mutual respect. You cannot expect to earn someone's trust by simply telling them you are trustworthy. You must demonstrate your trustworthiness over time. Likewise, respect is demonstrated over time after a series of contacts.

Effective coaches establish positive relationships with the teachers who they work with. How those relationships are developed is the subject of nearly every book ever written on coaching. There are no instant relationships, but I would like to offer a dating analogy to guide you in accelerating and broadening the development of your relationships with teachers.

THE MIXER

Imagine you have seen the person of your dreams. This person works at the same place as you, but you do not know them. What would be a logical progression for developing a relationship with that person?

Every group, whether it is a business, church, or even a casual group of friends who just hang, has gatherings that involve group members, as well as people outside the group. These gatherings have different names depending upon the structure of the group. If it is an informal group of friends, the gathering may be called a party. Churches may call the gatherings fellowships. Businesses will many times call them mixers.

These types of gatherings allow people who are strangers to be introduced in a casual manner. In fact, one of the main purposes of such gatherings is to meet and become acquainted with new people. Everyone attending understands that the main goal of the event is to meet new people, therefore attendees are open to being approached by and introduced to others.

Because you are playing the long game, your initial goal in meeting the person of your dreams is limited. You want to make a good first impression and let them know you exist. Most of the conversation you have should be focused on learning more about them. You can talk a little about yourself, but just a little. This is not the time to profess your undying love or to show them a vision board with pictures of your dream boat with them photoshopped into an image depicting your ideal life.

Take a deep breath. Tell the person you were glad to meet them and that you hope to see them again sometime.

THE MIXER EQUIVALENT AT SCHOOL
There are analogous opportunities to meet staff in low stakes settings. One is the regular staff meeting. Many school staff meetings open with some type of warm-up, team building, or 'getting to know you' activity. Although many teachers do not like these (possibly including you), do not act on your initial instinct to dismiss it. Use this type of activity to meet others at a personal level. Don't be an ass. Don't dominate. Find out about the other person.

Another opportunity is if you are asked to present at a staff meeting. It is common for coaches to be asked to present short trainings at staff meetings. Use this as an opportunity to get to know your staff. Do not use this an opportunity to show everyone how smart you are. The best way to let smart people know how smart you are is to let them know you are aware of how smart they are. Try to tell them something they don't know, but don't be smug about it.

GETTING COFFEE

Getting coffee is perceived to be a low risk, no strings attached, initial type of one-on-one social, dating activity. What makes it low risk? It usually occurs during daylight hours. It usually lasts for a short period of time, many times with pre-set time limits. (Having a pre-set time limit for the meeting allows an awkward meeting to end gracefully.) And as an added bonus, if the meeting goes sideways no one needs to be upset about having made a big financial investment.

What can you do if your one and only declines your invitation for coffee? It is very rare that someone will refuse without presenting some type of excuse. Now is not the time for a hard sell. You are playing the long game. Graciously accept their refusal and say you hope to see them around.

THE GETTING COFFEE EQUIVALENT

There are workplace activities that are analogous to getting coffee, i.e. low risk and time limited commitments. One is to tell the person you met at the mixer that you will be seeing them at their PLC grade-level meeting, data meeting, or any equivalent type of setting where teachers meet without administrators present. Like getting coffee, this is a low-risk activity.

While at the meeting shut up and listen. You are not selling yourself. You are there to learn about others, not to talk about yourself.

Another getting coffee equivalent is to tell the teachers you met that you will be in all classrooms for short visits. Let her know you are there for only a few minutes, just like coffee.

This option is more like asking to go out for coffee because the teacher may say, 'There is no good time to visit. My class does not do well with interruptions.' Just as someone might refuse a coffee date. Now is not the time for a hard sell. Graciously accept their refusal and say you hope to see them around.

A GOOD BUZZ

At this point either one of two things has happened. One, you have had coffee. Or two, your invitation was declined. Let's address the second option first: you got shot down for coffee.

This strategy assumes the other person, the object of your pursuits, does not appear interested. That person is just one of many in your company. To be in the position you have attained you must have lots of fans and admirers. This is the time to recruit them for your efforts.

Do you think the object of your pursuits might be affected by influential people in the workplace singing your praises? You need others to say nice things about you. These folks can say nicer things about you than you could have said about yourself.

If this works, the goal again is only coffee.

THE STRATEGY AT SCHOOL

After completing a coaching cycle post-observation meeting session, if a teacher volunteers that working with me was very beneficial, I say to them, 'Tell your friends!' And I mean it.

You need teachers with whom you have worked to vouch for you. You need them to tell others in the staff room (or in the PLC, grade-level meetings, or anywhere), that you are competent and respectful of teachers' time. That you are a true resource.

If this works, the goal again is coffee.

THE FIRST DATE

There is but one goal on the first date. To get a second date.

There will be no disagreements, no politics, no religion. Everything is good.

THE FIRST DATE: WITH THE TEACHER FOR REAL COACHING, THE COACHING CYCLE.

There is but one goal for the first date. To get a second date. Everything will be positive during the first coaching cycle.

SECOND DATE

Time to get to know the real you.

SECOND DATE: DEEPER COACHING

Real work begins.

FREQUENTLY ASKED QUESTIONS

Question: This seems like a lot. Is it all necessary?

Answer: It is only necessary when it is necessary. If you have already developed relationships with the teachers at a school, then you are good.

Question: I have never been comfortable meeting new people. Do you have any specific advice?

Answer: Be interested – a little. Beyond the dating analogy, here is an additional tip to help you develop relationships. You may end up 'dating', working together, quickly, or it may take a little more time. This advice holds for both circumstances.

The advice is simple. Most people appreciate it when others take an interest in them as people. Demonstrate interest in the other person by asking questions about them.

The most frequently asked question when meeting someone for the first time is, 'What do you do (for a living)?' Everyone who offers advice on how to be a good conversationalist strongly advises avoiding this question. Lucky for you, you won't make this mistake because you already know the person is a teacher.

What type of questions *should* you ask? Pay attention to conversations people are having in the staff rooms. These conversations provide clues about interests outside of school. Are they discussing plans for the weekend? Families? Hobbies? Be inquisitive. Ask follow-up questions that allow them to expand on their answers to those questions.

Notice personal pictures in classrooms. Do they have pictures of families, pets, vacations, hobbies? If the teacher has photos or other personal items displayed, you can ask about them. If such artifacts are not displayed, asking about family or outside activities should be avoided. Some people can judge such questions as invasive and creepy.

Does their clothing provide any insights into their interests? (Such as clothing with team logos, running shoes, exercise trackers, etc.). Ask questions, listen, smile, and leave information about yourself out of the conversation unless you are asked. This is about you learning about your colleagues and getting to know them.

When you encounter this colleague again you can inquire about their family or whatever you gleaned from your prior conversation. Your colleague will be impressed that you remembered some seemingly insignificant personal detail because most people don't do this.

It may be that making connections like this is something you naturally do. If you already do this, then you are familiar with the added benefit of people becoming more interested in you. As a coach you have a lot of professional conversations that need to happen. Personal connections should make those conversations easier.

Caution: As the first sentence of this answer states, Be Interested (*a little*). Don't be creepy. Seeming to be too interested by asking rapid fire questions can make people feel uncomfortable as if they just encountered a stalker or are being interrogated.

Remember: Coaching is based on long-term relationships.

Question: I have no problem developing relationships with staff members. Is this whole 'dating' thing really necessary?

Answer: The dating analogy is presented as a roadmap for people who are not as successful as yourself. Think of the suggestions as instructions for performing a task you already know how to do. You don't need to always use them, but they are there if you need them.

Question: I don't feel comfortable asking teachers about their personal lives. Do you have another strategy?

Answer: My initial reaction to this question is, 'You will probably need to do many things in your job as coach that you are currently not comfortable doing. The more you do it, the more comfortable it will become.' That being said, if you are visiting classrooms and you are paying attention there are always questions you can ask about lessons, displays, students, etc. My experience is that when you ask teachers these questions, they will divulge personal information that *they* are comfortable sharing.

CHOOSING THE FIRST COHORT FOR A COACHING CYCLE

Big Ideas:

- Get to know your teachers.
- Strive for heterogeneity.
- Choose gregarious Goldilocks.

OVERVIEW

Following the principal's proclamation, *all* of the teachers are expecting to meet with you for a coaching cycle. Having every teacher know they will be meeting with you makes choosing the first cohort easier, but not simple. It is easier because you are not asking for the teacher's 'permission' to meet with you. It is complicated because you still need to carefully consider who is the best group to start with. Either way, all the considerations about who to select to go first still apply.

'Okay wise guy. How do I choose the first group of teachers to work with?'

'Very carefully, Grasshopper. Very carefully.'

Only partly kidding. Maybe more accurately, choose strategically.

GET TO KNOW YOUR TEACHERS

Before you select your first cohort you need to get to know them as teachers. The first step is to visit every teacher's classroom. You don't need to be in their classrooms for an extended period of time to make a judgement about the teacher's openness to observers, evidence of classroom procedures, evidence of effective strategies (areas of focus), and general instructional competence. A brief visit gives only a snapshot of the teacher, but a snapshot is all you need when choosing your first cohort.

MAKE THE GROUP HETEROGENEOUS

Your first cohort should be so heterogeneous that no one should be able to look at the group and identify them as strong teachers, struggling teachers, new teachers, or [fill in the blank] teachers, etc. In one district that I worked in the principal selected an initial cohort that was composed entirely of special education teachers. This presented two problems moving forward in this district. First, the rest of the staff judged the coaching to be most appropriate for teachers of students with special needs. And second, the special education department was viewed by the rest of the staff as being comprised of low performing teachers. This double whammy made it difficult moving forward with the rest of the staff.

Do not choose groups who may be identified by the rest of the staff as the perpetual early adopters and/or those who are overly enthusiastic about anything new. The same warning applies to those who are perceived to have special skills, or particular interests, e.g. techies or big classroom personalities. All these considerations prevent teachers from generalizing the coach's work.

GREGARIOUS GOLDILOCKS

Your first cohort should include teachers who will be 'okay' to work with. Okay to work with means that they are open to meet with you but will communicate disagreements honestly and do not want their time wasted. Okay does not mean they can't be a little testy. They have high expectations for themselves, their students, and absolutely for you. Okay teachers will engage with you, and they will challenge you, but they will do so respectfully. Okay teachers are like Goldilocks; not too easy, not too hard.

Your first cohort should include talkers. And not just any talkers – those who have some influence with other teachers. Imagine the impact when you successfully work with a teacher who has a reputation for being a little hesitant to try something new and then shares what a positive experience it was working with you. If that teacher has any following in the teachers' lounge, then you will have done something extremely positive to advance your coaching efforts at your school. That is exactly the type of teacher you want in your first cohort.

You want teachers who are perceived as good, but cautious about trying new things. If your cohort has a couple of teachers like that then it is okay to have a couple of struggling teachers. It will also be okay to include an early adopter.

The first cohort of teachers should wield some influence over other staff members. They may have influence over many staff members, or only a few. Just be sure that these teachers are talkers. If they have a positive experience with you, they will let others know.

FREQUENTLY ASKED QUESTIONS

Question: How many teachers should I include in the first and then in subsequent cohorts?

Answer: Four or five is a nice-sized group. It big enough to be noticed by the rest of the staff, but small enough to make scheduling manageable.

Question: A teacher who doesn't fit your criteria has expressed a strong interest in being in the first cohort. Would it be okay to include this teacher?

Answer: Of course! If someone is excited about being coached, welcome them to the group.

PART THREE
COACHING CYCLES

PRE-OBSERVATION: PLANNING THE LESSON

Big Ideas:

- Structure the meeting.
- Work one-on-one.
- Get them talking (a protocol of respect).
- Resistant teachers.
- It is their lesson.
- Facilitating the planning process.
- Maintain focus through questions.
- Lesson plans don't need to be perfect.
- Special cases.
- Things not to say.
- Don't generalize too much.
- Last words.

OVERVIEW

The pre-observation planning meeting is a much-overlooked opportunity for coaches to become professionally acquainted with teachers. Coaches miss the golden opportunities the pre-observation meeting affords by rushing through it or seeing it as perfunctory. Missed opportunities occur due to lack of structure, coaching experience, or emotional understanding of the process, and/or a fear of face-to-face interactions with teachers.

Done well, the pre-observation conference provides an opportunity for the coach to engage a teacher with questions that they have which have arisen since their initial training. The pre-observation provides an opportunity for the teacher to participate in an open discussion about instruction that very rarely occurs in other venues. It allows coaches to gauge the level of buy-in from the teacher for the school's initiatives.

Pre-observation meetings will vary based on the experience and receptivity of the teacher being coached. As stated earlier, the principal can get every teacher to a coaching cycle which includes the pre-observation meeting. But it is up to the coach to make all the coaching interactions they have with teachers beneficial.

It has been my experience that all people are willing to work to improve. Without a coach it is very common for someone to work hard on the wrong things. A knowledgeable coach guides people to target the work that will be most important to accelerated improvement.

STRUCTURE THE MEETING

Every coaching activity is easier when there is an established routine, protocol, or structure. Establishing structures that can be replicated reduces the teacher's anxiety as well as yours. The routines stay the same, the teachers and their lessons change. As these routines become automatic, you can apply all your cognitive energy to the task at hand.

Here are some tips that help make everyone feel more comfortable.

CONTROL THE ENVIRONMENT

Meet somewhere other than the teacher's classroom. Meeting in the teacher's classroom is like working from home, there always seems to be some distraction. For example, the distraction might come from other staff who see the two of you meeting in the room. Because it is just the two of you, they feel it is okay to pop in for just a moment to ask a question.

Wherever you meet make sure there is a large whiteboard for your planning and note taking. It should go without saying, but make sure the markers are all working well. Pro tip: carry your own markers, and erasers. On the whiteboard write schoolwide instructional goals and anything else that your site has agreed should be included in the lesson.

The whiteboard, and the written goals then become the focus for both coach and teacher; physically and cognitively.[6]

The whiteboard is the physical focus because both the coach and teacher are looking in the same direction, at an object – the whiteboard. This eliminates the problem of the coach focusing on the teacher when asking questions. If the coach and the teacher are both looking in the same direction the process feels more collaborative and less interrogative.

By making the whiteboard the focus, both the teacher and coach are cognitively focused on creating something together. The focus is on what is written on the whiteboard and not on the teacher. Meeting with a coach should always feel like a collaborative effort.

By planning lessons on a whiteboard using erasable markers, the coach can model their thinking about collaborative lesson planning. Using a writing instrument that is easily erased makes it easy to modify initial ideas, make them better, and demonstrate how plans can evolve and be improved. If the planning occurs on paper changes can become messy. Even if the writing is done in pencil, erasures are difficult. It becomes

6   For the lesson goals shown on this white board see Pre-observation: Planning the Lesson, Planning a lesson with FAST.

easier to accept an inferior idea because it is too bothersome to eliminate a bad one.

Teachers will immediately want to take notes. I tell them I use erasable markers because things may change as we work through the lesson, and I don't want them to take notes if the lesson changes. Most teachers will take photos of the whiteboard after the lesson plan is completed.

SET A TIME LIMIT

Teachers should be informed prior to the meeting how long the pre-observation meeting will last. Before you begin, remind them of the time limit. Stick to that time limit. Sticking to the time limit demonstrates that you respect their time and them. Demonstrating respect for teachers is the best way for you to build strong and positive relationships.

Allocate and schedule 45-50 minutes for the planning session. This timeframe fits well with secondary teachers as that will match one class period. Even if the school is on a block schedule that may last as many as 90 minutes, stick to the 45-50 minutes. Elementary teachers are not tied to such rigid schedules but do have other scheduling issues such as recess, physical education, or other adjustments to a regular schedule.

When scheduling pre-observation meetings back-to-back to classes provide time in the schedule for teachers to get to and from their classrooms. This passing time helps reduce stress. Most teachers are very compliant and do not want to be tardy.[7]

STATE THE PURPOSE

Prior to the meeting, the coaching cycle process should have been explained to all the teachers in an email from the principal and the coach. Telling them the purpose of the meeting should be a reminder and an opportunity for teachers to ask any questions they may have about the coaching cycle.

The purpose of this meeting is to collaboratively plan a lesson which they will then be teaching the next day. However, I usually phrase it a little differently, a little softer. 'We are going to talk about a lesson you will be

---

7   It is very common for a teacher to arrive and immediately ask permission to use the restroom.

teaching tomorrow.' The reason I use the softer phrase, 'talk about', is that it is intentionally more ambiguous. The meeting can be very collaborative or not collaborative at all depending on the teacher.

Make sure the lesson being planned will be taught the next day, or the next time the class meets. Planning a lesson that will be taught the next day makes the process more real world and less performative. There are teachers who will spend hours and hours preparing for a lesson when they know they will be observed. If a teacher believes they need hours to prepare a single lesson, then teaching such lessons will not become habitual.

It should be noted that I disagree with asking teachers to choose what they want to work on during the coaching cycle. Until a baseline of competence has been established in the school's areas of focus, those are what everyone will be working on. Once that baseline has been established, school instructional priorities established, then coaching activities can progress to other areas.

WORK ONE-ON-ONE (AT LEAST INITIALLY)

It is best to work one-on-one when you initially meet with a teacher for a coaching cycle. There will be calls from administrators and teachers to have you work with groups (a group of teachers being more than one). Do not work with groups of teachers until you have met individually with each teacher who might potentially be in the group.

People behave differently in groups than they do individually. These differences can have negative effects has on others:

- In groups stronger personalities win. Whenever you have two or more teachers meeting together one of them will be dominant. I have never seen two teachers of equal expertise and personality. One teacher will always acquiesce.

- A stronger personality does not always have the best idea. Often, teachers who acquiesce have better ideas but know that they will never 'win'. They give up in the conversation but then later do what they want to do in the lesson anyway.

- Some stronger personalities may be negative, and their negativity can dominate the group. When you are meeting one-on-one with a negative teacher only one teacher is impacted. When you work with a group of teachers one dominant negative teacher impacts the entire group.

- Sometimes the negative teacher simply needs to be heard. A teacher who vents while meeting one-on-one provides you with an opportunity to learn about them without wasting the time of their colleagues. It may at first appear that you have wasted *your* time listening but allowing that teacher to be heard will positively impact your relationship with them in the long run. There are also teachers who are extremely negative but have no idea that they are perceived in that way. Arguing, or having a spirited discussion with that teacher in front of her colleagues may put that teacher in such a defensive position that you will never be able to establish a coaching relationship. Having a discussion, just the two of you, however, will not impact the teacher's self-esteem or self-perception of their status among colleagues.

- Less strong personalities may refrain from expressing their ideas, many of which might be awesome.

- Teachers have different needs, both professionally and emotionally. Just like students, teachers have different needs based on their experience and expertise.

GET THEM TALKING (A PROTOCOL OF RESPECT)

The only way to gather data about a teacher's ability to collaboratively plan an effective lesson is to get them talking. You learn much more when listening than when you are talking. You must get a handle on what the teacher is feeling about the process before you begin to plan. Ask questions that allow the teacher to express questions, concerns, and/ or their emotions about the entire process: 'Before we get started, do you have any questions about the training? Is there anything you need clarified? Is there anything you have implemented from the training? If you did, how did it go? Is there anything that you disagreed with? Or just anything you want to say?'[8]

---

8   As previously discussed, a general training should have occurred prior to the initial one-on-one coaching cycle. The purpose of the training is to present important content about the school's areas of focus.

I ask these questions in quick succession in the format above to demonstrate randomness, i.e. anything goes. The purpose of asking so many questions is to let the teacher know what types of topics might be discussed. I have found that asking questions in this manner, providing possible prompts, promotes more response than a single open-ended question such as, 'Do you have any questions about the training?'

You are not looking for answers to specific questions so please do not think of the sample questions above as some sort of checklist or survey. The sole purpose of asking these questions is to initiate conversation, not to serve as an interrogation.

Asking the questions all at once gives a teacher the opportunity to respond on a variety of topics. Most teachers have something positive to say about the training and express a desire to learn more. If a teacher does have a question about something from the training, or anything else, you have two options about providing an answer. If the question can be answered quickly you can choose to give an immediate answer. Or you can choose to respond to the question during the lesson planning if the planning process will provide additional context to better answer her question. If you choose this option, be sure you explain that to the teacher, so that she does not think you are dismissing her question.

The most important thing is that the teacher is talking about things that are interesting to them. This allows the coach to conduct the planning meeting with a slant towards the teacher's interests.

RESISTANT TEACHERS

There are teachers who will accept the invitation to express their disagreement and/or displeasure about some aspect of the training and/or meeting for coaching cycles. The schools that hire me typically choose teacher directed first instruction as the school's area of focus for instructional improvement. Although the research is clear regarding the effectiveness of teacher directed instruction, not everyone 'agrees' with the research.

Once during an initial meeting with a teacher, she expressed her displeasure with the school's choice for instructional focus (teacher directed instruction). To punctuate her displeasure she said, 'When Madeline Hunter died, I baked a cake and brought it to school to celebrate.'[9]

It may not feel like it when it is happening, but clearly expressed negative opinions are great time-savers. Direct conversations about such issues must occur. Although it is not your job to engage in extended debates with teachers, you should be able to defend your school's areas of focus. Not to discuss a teacher's reservations is disrespectful as everyone is entitled to their opinions. Such an exhibition of disrespect in the first one-on-one interaction can permanently damage any future opportunities to develop a collegial relationship.

Although it does not happen frequently, you will encounter teachers who will challenge being coached, the school's area of focus, and, in some cases, your personal credentials to be the coach. Most times when teachers express such concerns they just want to be heard. They need to vent.

Very rarely, a teacher goes even further and will flat out refuse to participate in the lesson planning process. There are usually two reasons. Some teachers have been presented with a curriculum that is designed to be implemented verbatim. Or the teacher simply rejects the entire coaching cycle process. I use a similar strategy to work with both.

The most important thing is to listen to and understand the teacher's objections. After I believe I have clearly understood the teacher's objections, I attempt to answer or mitigate their concerns. Most times we can get back on track. If we don't, at some point I will ultimately judge that the pre-observation planning will not happen.

Just because the planning did not occur does not mean that the coaching cycle will not happen. In these instances, I tell the teacher, 'When I come in tomorrow, just do what you always do; what you were going to do anyway. I will have an opportunity to see what you always do. We can talk about that during our post-lesson meeting. What are you teaching tomorrow?' Then I just listen.

When the teacher is done talking, we say goodbye.

---

9   This anecdote was reported to me by Dr. Frank Rodrigues.

PLANNING THE LESSON: GET AN OVERVIEW

You have an agenda. The coach's job during the pre-observation planning meeting is to collaboratively plan a lesson that includes the school's areas of instructional focus. Although it should be a truly collaborative process, both the process and the lesson belong to the teacher. The initial introduction to the process must reflect that.

I say something like, 'We are going to use a specific process to talk about your lesson, but before we do that can you give a thumbnail description of what you plan to teach tomorrow?'

At this point I am looking for generalizations about the lesson, not a lot of details. The details will come later.

Frequently I will interrupt the teacher, smile, and tell the teacher, 'I forgot to tell you I might be rude.' Most teachers return the smile and say that it's fine if I am rude. 'Let me tell you how my rudeness will manifest. See how I interrupted you as you were telling me about your lesson? That is how I will be rude. I am interested in everything you have to say about your lesson, but not right now. Because we have a limited amount of time, I might interrupt occasionally to ask clarifying questions.' Most teachers smile again and say that is fine.

I don't remember where I learned this communication tip, but it has proven to be very useful, 'You can tell anyone anything if you are smiling'. Smile a lot.

After the teacher has given an overview, I will step to the whiteboard to begin the collaboration. I tell the teacher I am going to interpret what they said about their lesson into a lesson framework that I have found useful in planning all types of lessons.[10] Whatever framework you use, the instructional areas of focus should be embedded in it. If a school's instructional areas of focus cannot fit into the framework, the school needs to change their areas of focus, or you need a new framework.

---

10   In schools where I coach it has been agreed that teachers will learn the FAST Framework, a teacher directed model of instruction. See Gene Tavernetti, *Teach FAST* (2022).

Before planning the lesson, I tell the teacher I am going to model a time saving lesson planning method that utilizes backwards planning. There is nothing earth shatteringly unique about backwards planning. In fact, most teachers know about it and are open to it, but have never been trained in how to use it.

To provide a detailed explanation of the process I am going to provide three examples of the backwards planning process. The first example of the process is using the FAST Framework as the school's area of instructional focus. The second example is using effective checking for understanding, students answering questions using complete sentences, and students interacting with other students. And finally, using a commercially prepared lesson.[11] In all three examples, the terminology as well as background knowledge that will be used during the planning meeting would have been introduced during the initial training.

EXAMPLE 1: PLANNING A LESSON USING FAST

I begin by asking the teacher clarifying questions about the lesson they have just described to me. These questions are chosen to model how to be more intentional when lesson planning. I use the lesson components from the FAST Framework to structure the conversation while using a backwards planning order. Below are the components, listed in planning order, with the questions I ask the teacher about each component. Also included is my thought process when planning a lesson.

#1 Learning Objective

What is your learning objective for the lesson?

A point of emphasis in the training is that lessons should have *one* objective. Many times, a teacher will list multiple objectives for a lesson. At this early stage of the planning process, I write down all objectives provided by the teacher without comment (we will circle back later).

#2 Independent Practice

What will you have the students do to demonstrate that they have accomplished the learning objective?

---

11 Commercially prepared lessons include those found in textbooks and various digital platforms (or generated by AI).

The learning objective and independent practice should match exactly. I ask the teacher to show me what the students will be asked to do. General responses like, 'I am going to have the students do the problems in the book,' are not acceptable answers at this time because textbook publishers are infamous for providing problem sets that include problems that have not been taught. There are times that a teacher has not brought materials to the planning meeting. Matching the learning objective to the independent practice is so important that in these cases I ask teachers to go back to their rooms to get materials.

After clarifying what students will be doing for independent practice, we do a quick check to ensure the learning objective still matches the independent practice. It is not unusual that the learning objective is modified after analyzing the match.

#3 Key Ideas

What are the new concepts that will be taught in this lesson?

The guiding question is, 'What is new in this lesson?' Concept development is one of the most often overlooked lesson components. Every lesson should include declarative concepts (the what), and/or conditional concepts (the when). Because many teachers shortchange this component, they initially have difficulty identifying what the conceptual knowledge in the lesson is. I don't belabor the point at this time. The lesson planning process will allow us to revisit these concepts in a moment (the teacher and I will circle back later).

#4 Expert Thinking (Modeling)

How do you do _____ (whatever the learning objective is)?

Many teachers will begin to respond by saying, 'What I tell the students is…' As soon I hear that phrase, I interrupt them, smile, and say, 'See how I was rude there? See how I interrupted you? Let me clarify my question. I am not asking what you are going to tell the kids. I am asking how *you* perform this skill?' They are always taken back by that comment. This is the time to model expert thinking; the teacher is the expert.

To clarify what I am asking I select one of the problems from the set the teacher provided for independent practice. While the teacher completes the task, I record what they did, i.e. the procedure used by the teacher to solve the problem.[12] After she is done with the problem, she verifies the procedure as I recorded it. I then say, 'That is what you will tell the students.'

Now that the teacher has produced a procedure, I have them look at it closely to determine if there are any concepts embedded in it that need to be taught. There should be. For example, the teacher may be planning a writing lesson in which students revise writing by using the 'show not tell' adage. One of the initial steps in making such a revision is finding forms of the verb 'to be'. Consequently, the various conjugated forms of the verb 'to be' are a concept that needs to be taught or reviewed.

We then circle back to the Key Concepts section to make sure any concept that the students need to know was included (in this example, the forms of the verb 'to be').

#5 Review

Is there anything in the procedure that was previously taught that needs to be reviewed?

Students have many learning gaps. By analyzing the procedure for solving problems in the independent practice problem set, a teacher can pinpoint exactly what needs to be reviewed, and in exactly what context. The review occurs by asking students to perform a skill that was previously taught.

Note: The procedure used to model (in Expert Thinking) provides guidance for what needs to be included in Key Ideas and in the Review.

#6 Guided Practice

Students should begin to practice immediately after the teacher models. But their practice should not address an entire problem. Gradual release should take place over three problems.

How do we break the procedure down to provide a gradual release of responsibility from teacher to students? For example, in the first practice problem the teacher will direct students to perform a single step and then

---

12   Procedures are most common in English language arts and math lessons. See *Teach FAST* (2022) for expert thinking in social studies and science lessons.

stop. After the teacher checks the students' work the teacher directs the students to perform the next step. The teacher and students perform the remaining steps one at a time until the process in complete.

In problem two, the teacher will direct students to perform more of the work before the teacher checks it. For example, the teacher may direct the students to do steps 1 and 2 and stop. Then steps 3 and 4 and stop. During the planning process, the teacher will be asked to plan which steps should be combined before checking.

And finally, for problem number three, students are directed to do the entire problem on their own.

#7 Closure

Most teachers do not do closure because they over complicate it. Closure is the teacher's final check for understanding. It occurs immediately after guided practice and immediately before independent practice.

Closure should include a question about the learning objective. Something as simple as, 'What was the learning objective?' It should also include at least one question from the Key Ideas component. Finally, the closure should include a question from guided practice.

#8 Anchor (Preview)

What is a question you could ask that connects students prior experience to the new concept in this lesson?

This will be the first thing the teacher will say in the lesson, but it is the last component planned. It is the last thing planned because it should directly relate to what will be taught, and the manner it will be taught later in the lesson. Using the above example of 'show don't tell', the teacher might ask, 'What does a very tall person do when he walks through a door?' Trying to determine the Preview prior to planning the lesson is usually a waste of time.

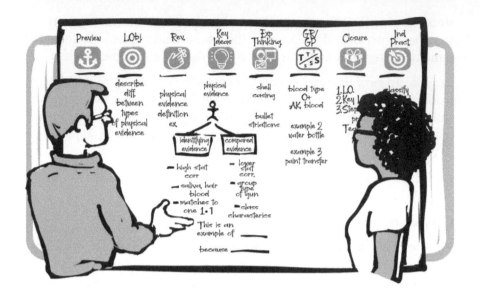

EXAMPLE 2: PLANNING A LESSON BASED ON AREA OF FOCUS

If you are coaching in a school that has not adopted a common lesson structure it is still possible to collaboratively plan a lesson. The school may not have a prescribed lesson structure, but you should have selected one for your coaching sessions.

Just as there are non-controversial and evergreen areas of instructional focus, there are also non-controversial and evergreen lesson structures and manners of lesson planning. The most common and helpful when planning a lesson is the idea of backwards planning, i.e. planning with the end in mind.

For this example, I will use the non-controversial and evergreen instructional areas of focus mentioned earlier. They are:

1. Effective checking for understanding.
2. Increasing student engagement.
3. Increasing student-to-student interaction.
4. Increasing students speaking in complete sentences.

The thread that ties the above areas of focus together is that the teacher must ask well-formed, intentional questions throughout the lesson. The teacher must also employ a variety of questioning strategies to ensure all students learn the content. A teacher who says she will use mini white boards to check students' responses to questions without also stating what questions will be asked has an incomplete lesson plan.

As in the prior example, ask the teacher for a short description of the lesson, after which you will ask questions to focus the discussion of the lesson. Specifically, you will ask how the areas of instructional focus will be applied. Many times, these questions will prompt the teacher to think about how and when the areas of focus might be embedded into a lesson in ways and places that they had not considered before.

#1 What is your objective for the lesson? How do you communicate that learning objective to the students?

Areas of focus questions: Do you have the students read the learning objective aloud? Do you practice pronouncing words in the learning objective that may be difficult? Do you have students tell a partner what the learning objective is? … 'Do you …?' Prompt the teacher to think about things she could do.

#2 How do you engage students at the beginning of the lesson?

Areas of focus questions: Do you have a 'do now', a problem or prompt on the board that the students do immediately upon entering the class? Do you ask a question that all students are able to answer, e.g. 'Have you ever gone to bed but couldn't fall asleep? Have you ever been late to school?' Do all students have a designated partner to share answers?

#3 What will the students do at the end of the lesson to prove they were successful?

Areas of focus questions: Do you inspect the questions or prompts to ensure they match what you will be teaching?

#4 How do you plan to present the new information in the lesson?

Areas of focus questions: Will you be using a concept map? Will you be using a language frame to help students articulate answers? Do you leave the language frame on the board? What questions should the students be able to answer? Have you included the questions in your presentation, so you won't forget to ask them? Do you have students do a 'pair share' with a partner before calling on individual students to answer? These questions prompt the teacher to think about strategies she might use.

#5 Do you need to review anything before you teach this lesson?

Areas of focus questions: How do you know students are successful doing the review? Do you use whiteboards?

#6 Will you be modeling during the lesson?

Areas of focus questions: Will your model include a procedure? Will your model include a concept map? What questions will you ask to ensure the students understand the concept map? Will the students be using language frames to help them articulate answers using complete sentences? Will students use whiteboards? Do you ask students to explain answers to a partner?

#7 Will you be facilitating student practice?

Areas of focus questions: How will you check your students' work? Do you have questions prepared for students to answer? Will students use a language frame to help them articulate answers?

#8 How do you know when the students are ready to work independently?

Areas of focus questions: Do you have a consistent routine for closing lessons, i.e. types of questions and procedures that prompt the students to engage with a partner to share what they have learned?

EXAMPLE 2: PLANNING A LESSON BASED ON A COMMERCIALLY PREPARED LESSON

In this final example the teacher has decided to use a commercially prepared lesson. Most lessons of this type provide the teacher with a prepared slide deck and often have videos, activities, or other digital resources.

The same questions asked in the above example will be asked during this pre-observation meeting.

1. What is your objective for the lesson? How do you communicate the learning objective to the students?
2. How do you engage students at the beginning of the lesson?
3. What will students do at the end of the lesson to prove they were successful?
4. How do plan to present the new information in the lesson?
5. Do you need to review anything before you teach this lesson?
6. Will you be modeling during the lesson?
7. Will you be facilitating student practice?
8. How do you know when students are ready to work independently?

Although you will be asking the same questions, the answers will come from the prepared lesson. As you ask the questions the teacher should be reviewing the prepared lesson to find answers to your questions. These questions serve as a checklist for the teacher to determine the completeness of the commercially prepared lesson.

The most neglected things in such lessons are the questions that will satisfy the areas of focus. In this case these are 1) effective checking for understanding, 2) increasing student engagement, 3) increasing student-to-student interaction, and 4) increasing students speaking in complete sentences.

LESSON PLANS DON'T NEED TO BE PERFECT

Most new coaches find the pre-observation meeting the most difficult part of the coaching cycle. The coach experiences a continuous internal struggle between contributing too much and too little. Experience is the only way to overcome this Goldilocks dilemma. The good news about the lessons you plan is that they do not have to be perfect.

There are some coaches who want the lesson plans to be perfect. Lesson plans can never be perfect because each lesson contains multiple unknown variables, namely, the students. In some ways I prefer lessons to be a little rough around the edges. Instruction is not about perfection; it is about real time adjustments based on formative data. Pre-observation planning is just one-third of the cycle. Let things go.

SPECIAL CASES

COACHING OUT OF CONTENT AREA

Depending on your specific title and job description you may be asked to coach teachers who teach content outside what you would consider your area of expertise. Most elementary schools have a single coach. Many secondary schools have a single coach to serve teachers in all content areas. Take a deep breath and tell yourself, 'I can be an effective instructional coach outside of my content area.'

If you are an instructional coach in grades K-8 you need a dose of reality. You have a college degree, possibly a graduate degree. You can handle any content a 12- or 13-year-old is required to learn. Just stop saying, 'I am not a math person,' or whatever the content area you do not feel expert in is.

Earlier in this book the principal's role in the coaching program was clearly laid out. One of the primary responsibilities of the administration is to provide an instructional focus that is non-controversial and evergreen. Your primary responsibility as the coach is to ensure that those areas of focus are maintained in all classrooms.

Imagine the focus of the school is to increase the amount of academic student talk in its classrooms. How much do you need to know about plate tectonics to coach a geography teacher in increasing student talk? In most cases the area in which you are supporting teachers is not their content but in strategies that increase instructional effectiveness in all classrooms.

That these strategies may look different across classrooms is not a function of the content area, but of the behavioral norms that have been established in each classroom, the existing classroom culture, and the personality of the teacher.

If you are working in grades 9-12 you need a reality check. You are a college graduate. You may not feel like an expert, but you can certainly understand the content being taught. More importantly, you are not there to demonstrate the latest or most popular trends regarding content.

Most school districts have content area specialists to support teachers. These content area specialists have different responsibilities than you. The specialists' jobs are to stay up to date on methods, strategies, cool new stuff, etc. If your district does have content area specialists, then you will soon discover who they are because you will be visiting every classroom. There may be some overlap with your responsibilities, but their jobs are content based, not the instructional, non-controversial, evergreen areas of focus established by the principal that are your responsibility.

Because I have coached teachers from grade levels K through 12, in all content areas, I have learned an amazing amount of content I missed when I was a student. I do not consider myself an expert in any content area. I do consider myself an expert in instruction. That is what I express to teachers. I tell them, 'I am not an expert in Calculus. You are an expert in Calculus. I am an expert in instruction.' I feel comfortable saying that. Come up with your own way of framing that sentiment in a manner that you feel comfortable with.

I never try to fake expertise. On the other hand, I may fake ignorance. Faking ignorance allows me to ask the teacher to expand and enhance an explanation. Unfortunately, I have encountered teachers who, like me, are also not experts in their content area. It is rare, but there have been times I have had to talk to a principal about a teacher who is teaching content that is not accurate.

You don't have to be an expert in all content areas, but you should be curious about what is being taught. When you are coaching out of your area read an article, watch a video. Learn a little bit more each time. You may not become an expert, but you will be far ahead of where you started.

You don't have to be an expert, but you *do* need to develop a network of experts in all the content areas who you can call on to support both you and the teachers. These are people who really are experts and who you can ask questions. They may be teachers or people who work in the field. Most times people are happy to talk about a subject they are passionate about.

COACHING A VETERAN TEACHER

If you wish to be understood, first seek to understand.

Stephen R. Covey, *The 7 Habits of Highly Effective People* (1989)

Many coaches feel anxious about meeting with a veteran teacher. It may cause you to be a little reticent, a little hesitant to be as forthcoming as you are with other teachers. Good. That means you have some good instincts and some good intuition that you should treat coaching a veteran differently. It does not matter what you think of a veteran teacher's ability to provide effective instruction, that teacher deserves total respect. However, that does not mean she deserves total deference.

What beliefs do you have about veteran teachers that make you think coaching them is different, more difficult, than coaching any other teacher? Do you believe they are more knowledgeable than you? Do you believe their veteran status makes them less likely to be open to being coached?

I have never convinced any teacher – veteran or novice – to try something different. Teachers make decisions to change on their own. If *never* can be even more definitive, that goes double for veterans.

Think back to a time when you were young and had a conversation with an adult who was much older such as a grandparent. You may have related a story about some current event in your life. You were so excited about some brand-new thing you personally discovered, some insight no one else knew. The older adult smiles, compliments you, and may even pat you on the head for your insight.

Their smile may be because they have lived through the same thing when they were younger. They compliment you because you had an insight. They remember how they felt when they were your age, excited about being the only one in the world to experience this new thing. They may pat you on the head because in that moment they realize you are growing up. The older person appreciates your wonder, but they know it isn't new or unique.

Many educators talk about the swinging pendulum. The pendulum swings because there is no institutional memory in schools. Something 'new' comes down the pike from parts unknown and every school and school district jumps on the bandwagon. There may be a lot of excitement from everyone except the veterans. For the veterans this is not new; this is not exciting. Whatever discussions are happening currently at your site, the veterans have lived through them before. Many times, they are even able to predict the future, or the outcome, of the latest initiative – they have seen it before.

The most important thing to remember when working with veteran teachers is to show them respect. How do you show respect for veteran teachers? To paraphrase Steven Covey's quote that started this section, do not offer any advice about anything until you become familiar with them.

You need to observe their classrooms to become familiar with their routines, methods, procedures, etc. before you meet with them for a coaching cycle. The observation should spur questions about what they are doing, how they developed a particularly effective routine, had they tried something different in the past, etc.

Do more listening than talking. You can only listen if they are talking, which means you need to ask lots of questions. Get them talking and listen closely to learn all you can about them. You are *not* gathering intel for a debate you intend to have with them later. You *are* gathering intel into their classroom practices.

Until you get to know a teacher and until you work with a teacher you do not know how they will react to coaching. Some of my most gratifying coaching sessions have been with veteran teachers. They appreciated that I didn't waste their time. Hopefully, they also appreciated that I was competent.

In many ways coaching veteran teachers is no different than coaching other teachers. Treat veteran teachers with respect. That is not different. Some teachers are more open to coaching than others, veteran or not. Get to know them, get to know their practice. As it is with all teachers, do not start making suggestions until you are familiar with them.

The length of time that a teacher has been teaching does not necessarily mean they are experts in all things pedagogical. Be respectful and do your thing.

COACHING NEW TEACHERS

The main piece of advice on how to coach veteran teachers is to show respect. When coaching new teachers, you must also show respect, but it will look different. Respect for new teachers manifests by recognizing and validating the teacher's experiences (or lack thereof), fears, and frustrations. The new teacher needs to know she is not alone. New teachers may not openly show their insecurities to the other staff members, but they do exist.

Another way to demonstrate respect is to not embarrass them by asking questions that they may not have answers to. For example, in contrast to veteran teachers, there are many lessons that new teachers have not taught. If it becomes apparent that the new teacher is unable to answer a question that was meant to guide her, help her out. In such a situation you should model how to find out what they need to know. There is no shame in not knowing, so don't make it shameful. Schedule a time to meet again. You are playing the long game. This is another piece of data regarding the needs of the teachers you coach. Is there some resource you can provide her? Are there other teachers who need similar assistance?

NOTES

During the pre-observation meeting it is important to let teachers know what to expect during the classroom observation. Tell teachers you will be taking notes while you are observing their lesson. In another section (DNBYOD – Do not bring your own device) I warn coaches not to bring computers or tablets into the classroom to take notes. If video is part of the teaching culture, then great, record the lesson. However, because recording the lesson may increase stress levels, I will forgo it until a more trusting relationship has been developed. On the other hand, it is important for coaches to keep a personal record of the lesson to provide the teacher with accurate feedback during the post-observation conference.

I use a simple notetaking structure. I note times, topics, student and/or teacher behaviors, and any commendations or tips I will want to share with the teacher during the post-observation meeting. I also note how the students responded. Ideally this will include a quote from either the teacher or a student. Providing an exact quote during the post-observation conference lets the teacher know how closely you were paying attention.

An example of my format is below (I used this same format when I was an administrator). Develop your own style and it will serve you well.

Time	Topic	What happening?	Commendations/tips
9:00	Preview	T-. ever seen a rainbow? Tell partner what remember. T calls on 3 students to share	All kids involved; effective transition to LO. "I heard several students say the rainbow was pretty, the rainbow had colors. Raise your hand if you said pretty, …colors. The words you used to describe the rainbow are adjectives and that is what we are learning"
9:03	Learning Obj.	T-reads. Ss reads. T helps Ss pronounce/ practice saying	Quick, effective
9:05	Review	Ss identify words from a list that are nouns	Ss doing the work

Most teachers imagine the worst when they see an observer taking notes. 'What did I do wrong?' 'What is she writing down?' Before you leave the pre-observation conference, show the teacher how you will take notes. This of course presupposes you have selected a method for taking notes. Giving the teacher a peek into your process helps assure her that you are looking for positive elements in the lesson.

Choose the method that works best for you. The only strong recommendation I have is not to use a checklist. Effective teaching is not about checking boxes. Using a checklist can give the teacher the impression you are not seeing her, or her students, as individuals.

A few warnings. I have worked with colleagues who wrote negative comments in their notes such as, 'I can't watch any more of this!! I want to poke my eyeballs out with pencils.' Do you know who may see your notes? Neither do I! Keep your comments objective and positive.

Be factual about what happened, be professional about comments and tips.

In the 15 years I have been coaching teachers I have only had one school object to me taking notes during lessons. In response to their objections, I explained that the purpose of the notes is to help me remember what happened during the lesson to help me provide better feedback to teachers. My reasons were irrelevant. They did not want anyone who observed their class taking notes. It seemed ridiculous to me until I found out the reason for their objection.

There was very little trust between the teachers and administration at this school. The teachers were afraid the notes would end up in the hands of the administration and be used as part of their evaluations. I reiterated my argument for taking notes: There are days that I may observe six lessons. It is nearly impossible for me to remember everything of note during all those lessons. Remembering everything that may have happened was made even more difficult because teacher reflection and debriefing typically did not occur on the same day as the observation.

There was nothing I could say, no explanation I could give about how the notes would be used, that could overcome the lack of trust that was being voiced. An agreement was finally reached that I could take notes during the lesson, but the notes would be relinquished to the teacher before the I left the classroom. We also agreed that whenever possible, the teacher's reflection and debrief would occur immediately after the lesson. These solutions were not optimal, but they kept the coaching on track.

As a side note, the teacher who objected the most was the union rep for the school. If you are ever in doubt about anything contractually, check with your principal.

FINAL THOUGHTS BEFORE THE TEACHER LEAVES

After the lesson has been planned, I ask the teachers if they have any questions about anything. When the teacher's questions have been answered, I always give two little pep talks.

The first is about the lesson we just planned. I point to the whiteboard that now contains the plan for the lesson to be observed. I tell them, 'We just spent 45 minutes on this lesson. Between now and the time you teach this lesson, you will probably have some ideas about something that may be done differently. Feel free to make any changes you want. Just because we wrote it on the board does not mean you have to do it that way. You are the boss! It is your lesson. If you want to change anything, go ahead, and change it. Do not feel like because we didn't talk about something you shouldn't do it.'

The second pep talk is regarding the goal of the observation. I tell teachers that the goal of the observation and coaching cycle is to do everything possible to ensure that the lesson goes well. I am not there to watch teachers struggle doing something new and then subsequently meet and tell them what they could have done better. This is especially true if I could have, just in time, given them a bit of advice to make the lesson go even better.

To that end, I say to the teachers, 'This is not a performance. The lesson is guided practice for you. I know that some things you will be trying in this lesson may be new, so if you have any questions during the lesson just look at me and ask, "What about this?" or any other questions that you might have. I will answer your question and if needed we can have a short conversation if you want further clarification about something.'

The final part of the pre-observation routine and pep talk is to ask the teacher permission to intervene in a positive manner during the lesson.[13] 'And on the other hand, if this is okay with you, if *I* see something that might be helpful, I will raise my hand and ask a prompting question like, "Do you think the students are ready to practice on their own?" The reason I bring it up is because I don't want you to see me with my hand up and you think something is wrong.' It is very rare that I do raise my hand in such a manner, but now I have their permission.

This type of intervention still produces valuable formative data for the coach regarding the teacher's performance and thinking during the lesson. I always tell new teachers that if they are being observed by an evaluator and something is not working, it is much better to acknowledge

---

13 A second time reader may argue this is a contradiction of the Prime Directive (see the next chapter: Observing Lessons). The Prime Directive applies to working with students.

that something is off, rather than trudging through an ineffective lesson.

Very rarely, a teacher will tell me that they would rather not be interrupted. In these cases, I tell them I am fine if they don't want me to do that.

Many teachers are used to the principal expecting to observe a lesson that lasts an hour. No instructional episode should last an hour. For most elementary classrooms, I tell them I will be leaving after about 30 minutes; plenty of time to teach a lesson. The last thing I tell the teacher is that when the lesson is over, I am leaving. 'Do not feel like you need to entertain me.'

FREQUENTLY ASKED QUESTIONS

Question: What should teachers do to prepare for the pre-observation planning meeting?

Answer: The minimum necessary preparation is to have selected a learning objective. Teachers should also bring any materials they plan to use such as a teacher's edition of the text, any handouts, or any digital materials they plan to use. (This expectation should all be laid out in an email from the principal and coach prior to the meeting.) I tell teachers if all they have is a learning objective, that is fine. If they have a completed lesson plan, that is also fine.

Question: What if a teacher wants to design a lesson that I have taught many times? Should I tell the teacher how I have taught it?

Answer: I have two responses. The first is no one cares how you used to teach the lesson! You used to be a teacher. Now you are something else.

But what if you really did a great job teaching that lesson? Instead of saying 'This is how I used to teach this.' Say this instead, 'I saw a teacher teach that lesson. This is what I saw her do.'

Is it a lie if the teacher you saw, was you? Only kind of sort of. At worst it is a little tiny white lie told to help a colleague. Are you disappointed the teacher won't know it was you who was the brilliant teacher? If you are, then maybe you shouldn't be a coach. If you want credit for being a good teacher, then go back to teaching. If you want credit for being a good coach, then help teachers get better.

My second response has to do with your goals for the pre-observation planning session. The goals are to model how to design a lesson, and to gather data about the teacher's knowledge of performing that task. If the teacher is truly stumped by all your guiding questions, then employ the advice provided above. Tell them, 'I saw a teacher …'

OBSERVING LESSONS

Big Ideas:

- Entering the room.
- Prime Directive.
- Smile.
- No devices.
- Exiting the room.

OVERVIEW

A primary goal during the observation is to make the teacher as comfortable as possible. The more comfortable the teacher is, the more accurate a reflection of their skills you will witness. The more accurate the reflection of skills is, the more accurate the data will be, and the better the resulting reflection and suggestions for improvement will be.

If it were possible, the best way to observe the lesson would be for you to be invisible. Since that is not possible, the next best thing is to follow the suggestions in this chapter. These suggestions have the goal of making you as invisible as possible and the teacher as comfortable as she can be, given the circumstances.

Advocating invisibility could be seen as an argument for watching a recording of the lesson versus an in-person observation. I think recording lessons is great, but the reality is that most teachers are as intimidated by being recorded as they are being observed. Also, if a teacher gets 'stuck' during the lesson then there is no one there to process the problem with.

ENTERING THE ROOM

Initially, most teachers will experience a negative emotional response to your presence in the classroom. Some teachers are apprehensive because they lack confidence. Others are anxious because they want to impress. Others have concerns for their students; they are afraid student learning will be disturbed. It is a rare teacher who could not care less about you observing them. Instead of guessing which category of teacher you are working with, plan your observation assuming that they will be anxious, and do everything that you can to mitigate that.

Do not arrive early. If you are scheduled in a classroom following a break do not enter the classroom until all the students have arrived and have had an opportunity to find their seats. This allows the teacher and students to handle the transition in their customary fashion.

If you are entering a classroom at a time other than transition (this occurs mostly in elementary grades), wait until your scheduled time to enter the classroom. It is possible that the teacher has already had to modify her usual schedule to accommodate your visit, don't add to the pressure by arriving early.

Do not expect that the teacher has prepared a special place for you to sit. Most secondary classes have a little extra room. Some teachers will provide a chair, but don't count on it. My preferred seating is at a student desk in the back of the room. This keeps me out of the line of sight of most students. If there is no vacant desk, I will move a chair to the back of the room. My personal comfort is the last thing I am worried about.

Do not engage the teacher in conversation. A subtle wave hello allowing the teacher to acknowledge your presence is a sufficient greeting. If the teacher needs to talk to you, or has a question prior to the lesson, let her engage you.

THE PRIME DIRECTIVE

If you are a fan of the Star Trek series, please excuse me as I paraphrase the Prime Directive under which Federation Starships operated when exploring the galaxy: do not interfere. If Federation ships visited a less advanced culture, they were to do so sub-rosa, as observers only, so as not to meddle with that society's development.

When observing a classroom, I obey the Prime Directive. Do not interfere with the students. For many coaches this is extremely difficult. If coaches observe one or more students struggling, they want to assist by providing one-on-one help to the struggling students. These coaches believe they must decide between the Prime Directive and a 'Hippocratic Oath' for teachers. Some coaches feel an almost moral obligation to provide help to the students.

Do not do it!

As a coach you are there to observe, collect data, and provide instructive and constructive feedback to the teacher.

Take off your teacher's hat and fight the urge to help that struggling student. When you provide support, you rob the teacher of the opportunity to provide support. You rob yourself of the opportunity to see if the teacher knows that the student is struggling, and you rob yourself of the opportunity to see how and when the teacher provides support.

If you intervene, you help the student once. If you support the teacher, you will be supporting all their future students.

Just as a teacher collects formative data about students' performance during lessons, a coach is collecting formative data about the teacher's performance. If the coach steps in to help a student, the coach robs themselves of the opportunity to observe the teacher respond to students in need.

Being a coach means you are helping teachers get better. You can only help them get better by observation.

SMILE

Many thoughts will be going through your head as you observe lessons.

'Wow! That was amazing!'

'If I was doing this lesson I would ... '

'I wonder if she knows that that student has had her hand up for over a minute?'

'If she would just say _____, the students would get it.'

'It is amazing how she has taught her students those effective classroom procedures.'

'I wonder if I could get her to share what she is doing at a staff meeting?'

All these thoughts and more will be going through your head. Some thoughts are very complimentary, some less so. The expression on your face could change based on whether what you are seeing is positive or negative. The expression on your face could change because you are deep in thought about what you might tell the teacher in your post-observation meeting. The expression on your face *could* change, but don't let it.

Every time the teacher looks at you, she should see a smile. If the teacher sees a look of consternation, it could trigger a reaction that may impact what she does in the lesson. Regardless of experience, teachers will experience some anxiety about having you in their classroom observing lessons. Realize that the teacher will also be observing you, attempting to discern your reaction. Your reaction should always be the same – a smile.

As you begin to visit and observe more teachers and more lessons you will soon realize there is some funky stuff going on in some of your colleagues' classrooms. Stuff that you would have never believed if you hadn't seen it with your own eyes. You will observe things that may even border on malpractice.

When you go into a classroom to observe a lesson that is less than optimal for students you will know that in a matter of minutes. When you were a teacher, you were probably upset with administrators who would drop by for just a few minutes. You wondered how they had the nerve to provide any type of feedback, even positive feedback, after such a small sample size.

The reality, which you will come to know, is that a competent observer can determine a lot in just a few minutes. A competent observer can watch a lesson and infer what happened before they arrived, predict what will happen in the next few minutes, and imagine what will occur after they are gone.

You are not an administrator doing a quick drop in and staying for only a few minutes. When you observe you should watch entire lessons. That means that there will inevitably be times when you will observe a lesson that you knew was bad three minutes after you walked in. You don't get to leave.[14] You must watch the entire lesson. You must watch the entire lesson and you must smile.

While you are sitting observing, bathing in your reverie, there is a nervous, anxious teacher in the classroom sneaking peeks at you to try to get some clue about what you are thinking. Even in the best-case scenario where you are lost in thought about how to get everyone to see this wonderful teacher's practice, the look on your face may be one of 'What a challenge I have ahead of me.' The teacher is looking for feedback and all they see right now is your expression.

---

14 During the pre-observation conference tell the teacher that you will be leaving after 30 minutes. That should be enough time for any teacher to accomplish whatever the goal might be.

Make sure that every time a teacher sneaks a peek at your mug, she sees a smile.

DNBYOD (DO NOT BRING YOUR OWN DEVICE)

It is common practice these days for administrators and other observers to enter notes on a computer or tablet while observing lessons. If you feel the urge to bring your own device … *don't do it.*

When a teacher is being observed, regardless of what they tell you, their emotions will run from slightly anxious to a total nervous wreck. You need to do everything you can to help the teacher maintain her composure.

When you are entering notes on an electronic device the teacher will be diverting her attention away from teaching to wondering what you are typing. When you are entering notes on a device you are not paying attention to the teacher. There is no such thing as multitasking.

It has been my experience that it is usually administrators who use devices to take notes during observations. When I have spoken to them about it, their reasoning is it allows them to save time writing up observations because they do not have the extra step of transcribing notes. The purpose of observation is to help the teacher, not to make your job easier.

Smile!

CREATIVE STRATEGIES

Once during an observation, a teacher began the lesson by saying to the students, 'Remember what I told you earlier.'

The teacher then asked a question about the lesson and waited for hands to go up. Only a few students responded. He repeated the question and again said, 'Remember what I told you earlier.' This admonition did not result in any more hands being raised in response to his question.

Later, during the last part of the coaching cycle, the reflection and debrief, I asked the teacher what he had wanted the students to remember. He chuckled and said, 'I told them when I asked a question, I wanted everyone to raise their hands as if they knew the answer. If they knew the answer, they should raise their right hand. If they didn't know the answer, they should raise their left hand. I told them I would only call on students with their right hand raised.' Sometimes teachers will try to fool administrators, coaches, or others.

EXITING THE ROOM

During the pre-observation meeting I tell teachers that when the lesson is over, I will leave. When the lesson is over, I stand up as unobtrusively as possible, make eye contact with the teacher, and wave goodbye. I usually silently mouth something easily understood even by non-lip readers like, 'thank you', or 'good job'.

Smile!

FREQUENTLY ASKED QUESTIONS

Question: Should I intervene if a student is misbehaving?

Answer: No, unless it is a safety issue. And even then, think invisibility.

POST-OBSERVATION

Big Ideas:

- Structure.
- Set a time limit.
- Three question protocol.
- Additional rationale for these three questions.
- Gestalt of the three questions.
- There is no need to embarrass.
- Limit your suggestions.
- Check for understanding.
- You can't tell them everything you know.
- Talking so that teachers will listen.
- Power phrases.
- Last words.

OVERVIEW

It is very common for new coaches to view the post-observation meeting as downright scary. They have questions about how to begin the conversation about the observed lesson. They worry about how teachers will react to negative feedback. They are afraid teachers will react badly to any type of feedback. Having a plan with specific goals can help allay these fears significantly.

The coach's goals for the post-observation meeting are to celebrate what was effective in the lesson, give insightful feedback, and help teachers identify goal(s) for improvement. Contrast those objectives with the teacher's goal which is to end this stressful experience as soon as possible.

The stress response will prevent the teacher from remembering much of the feedback you give. The purpose of this chapter is to help minimize the new coach's trepidation and reduce the teacher's stress to maximize retention of your suggestions.

Some of the suggestions in this chapter are very concrete and should be implemented immediately (e.g. set a 10-15 minute time limit, limit suggestions, check for understanding, three questions). Others – such as the communication strategies (talking so teaches will listen, power phrases) – are somewhat sophisticated and subtle. Although they are useful, it is not necessary to have mastered them before you begin coaching cycles.

STRUCTURE THE CONFERENCE

Every coaching activity is easier when a protocol or a structure has been established. The same rationale that was used for structuring the pre-observation applies to the post-observation conference. Establishing structures that can be replicated eases your anxiety as a coach which will be reflected in the teacher's response. The structure stays the same, the teachers and lessons change. As the structures become automatic and your fears diminish, you can exert more of your cognitive energy on the task at hand, helping teachers improve.

SET A TIME LIMIT OF 10-15 MINUTES

Parkinson's Law states that work expands, or contracts, based on the time allotted. Setting a time limit, especially such a short one, creates a sense of urgency for everyone to begin the work at hand. This sense of urgency gives you permission to limit what is generally considered to be polite small talk.

People can withstand more pain if they know how long the pain will last. If a teacher knows the post-observation reflection and feedback meeting is only going to last for 10 minutes, she can remind herself, 'How bad can it be?'

To let the teacher know I am serious about the time limit, I make a big theatrical production of grabbing my phone and setting an alarm. After greeting the teacher and a few moments of pleasantries, I say, 'Oh, I almost forgot. Let me set a timer for 10 minutes otherwise we will just keep chatting.' The timer gives you permission to keep the conversation focused. The time limit gives you an excuse to wrap up the meeting.

You will work with teachers who appreciate the support you provide or who simply love you. If they could spend all day with you, they would. Listen to what the teacher has to say. Say what needs to be said and then say good-bye.

Some teachers are just the opposite and are more resistant to the process. Resistant teachers may act aloof and non-responsive. Or they could even be outright hostile. Hostility is preferable to silence. At least you got the teacher talking.

Resistant teachers are usually veteran teachers. Over the years they have had so much of their time wasted by various initiatives it is likely the animosity they are displaying is aimed at someone else from their past and not you. That is unless you are also wasting their time, then it is aimed at you.

If you are competent, if you have done a good job with the pre-observation conference and observation, you may find the resistant teacher will begin to come around to your side – a little. Competence matters.

In either case, the timer becomes your best friend. As stated above, people can withstand pain if they know how long it will last. Sometimes the pain the timer will be ending is your own. Set a timer.

THREE QUESTION PROTOCOL

Incorporating a routine, or protocol, into every post-observation meeting, relieves the pressure of deciding how to begin. Every teacher is unique. Every lesson is unique. The structure of each conference is the same, but the individuals and the lessons will make each post-observation unique.

My routine for initiating the post-observation meeting is always the same. I tell the teacher, 'I have three questions for you. You can answer them in order, not in order, holistically, however you want.'

These are the three questions I ask all teachers … well nearly all teachers. (More on that later.)

1. How do you think the lesson went?
2. Did you do anything different than what we had planned? (If it was a secondary teacher who taught the lesson multiple times, I would add, 'How did you change the lesson throughout the day'.)
3. What would you do differently next time?

Ask the questions and then shut up and listen. I have one exception to this rule. If a lesson went very well and the teacher begins her response with, 'I think it went okay' then I will interrupt and say, 'I disagree! It was way, way better than okay.' If someone else also observed the lesson, I will turn to them and let them echo the positive comment (I know the comment will be positive because we will already have discussed the lesson prior to the meeting). These comments provide the celebration alluded to earlier. I apologize to the teacher for the interruption and tell her to continue. This interruption to compliment helps put the teacher at ease. Teachers tend to be very self-critical and may have genuinely believed the lesson did not go well. Teachers tend to be more forthcoming, a little less critical of their lesson, if they realize I evaluated it more positively.

A teacher may also be self-deprecating as a self-defense mechanism. It is very possible that the teacher thought their lesson went very well but is hesitant to be the first to say so just in case I have a different opinion.

The first time a meet with a teacher after a lesson, it seems they expect to be heavily criticized. I am not sure what their prior experiences with a coach or administrator were, but they expect to hear one criticism after another. This defensive posture can be overcome with a simple compliment. Telling the teacher up front I think the lesson went well lowers the teacher's affective filter. They are already anxious, so do everything you can to make the post-observation meeting a positive experience.

Answering the second question – did you do anything different than what we had planned? – allows the teacher to speak specifically about how she reflects on her teaching. Many teachers are good at diagnosis but not treatment. Luckily for them you are good at both.

The last question – what would you do differently next time? – also allows teachers to be reflective. Like the second question, the teacher's response provides information about their ability to evaluate her own lesson. The teacher's response will help to guide feedback. It makes no sense to talk about the subtleties if a teacher does not recognize that more major adjustments are necessary.

ADDITIONAL RATIONALE FOR THESE THREE QUESTIONS

Q1: How do you think the lesson went?

Developing a trusting relationship with the teacher is important. I am hoping to learn a few things about the teacher. The first question provides a way to gauge if the teacher feels comfortable enough to provide an honest assessment. It allows me to gauge the teacher's level of defensiveness, the accuracy of her self-assessment, and what they judge to be important in a lesson.

One big caveat, I only ask this question if the lesson was not a total disaster. If the lesson was a total disaster, I do not want a teacher telling me she thinks the lesson went well. What to say when the lesson was a total disaster will be addressed below in frequently asked questions.

Sometimes I couch the first question with one of the following statements (or something similar): 'Because I have never seen your class before.' Or, 'I have only been in your classroom a couple of times.' Or I follow up with 'How was today's lesson compared to other days?'

The origin of these qualifiers dates to my early days of playing golf. It goes without saying that as a beginner I was not very good. In golf, an important part of learning the game is the proper etiquette. There is an expectation that players compliment others' shots throughout the round. 'Nice drive.' Or, 'Great shot!' 'Nice putt!' 'Great up and down.' 'Nice birdie.'

One day I found myself playing in a group with someone I had not previously met. The other two players in the foursome were familiar with this fellow and his abilities. He was clearly the best player in the group, but also the strongest I had played up to this point.

After a few holes I realized that I was the only one in our group complimenting him on his shots. It turns out I was telling him 'Great shot,' on shots that would have been great for me but were not very good at all for him.

Telling someone 'Good shot' when it is in fact not a good shot could be perceived as slightly mocking. (As I became a more experienced golfer, I learned the proper comment on an okay shot is 'That will work.' But even that can be taken the wrong way. I can imagine a response like, 'That will work? Why don't you just say, "Bad shot"? That is what you were thinking.')

The point being, if you haven't seen a teacher present a lesson before it is best to ask her for some type of baseline.

Q2: Did you do anything different than what we had planned?

During the planning meeting I am modeling how to efficiently plan a lesson. I do this through guided questions. The lesson we designed is not necessarily the definitive way to teach the targeted objective. There is always something that might be done better.

During the process I continuously tell teachers, 'This is your lesson.' Even with constant reminders that it is their lesson, many teachers are extremely deferential and think it is best if they just do what I suggest.

If a teacher only does what I say or follows every suggestion I made while planning, the lesson becomes my lesson and not the teacher's. If the lesson does not go well the teacher does not need to take responsibility. If the lesson didn't work, it was my fault.

Before the pre-observation planning session ends, I tell teachers, 'I will get up tomorrow and will be thinking about this lesson. And there is always something about a lesson where I think, "We should have done this instead of that. Or this would have been better." Between now and tomorrow if you want to change something please feel free. This is your lesson. You are the boss.'

Always encourage self-reflection. Always encourage them to make things better.

Q3: What would you change if you taught this lesson again?

Again, the purpose of the question is to promote self-reflection. Lessons can always be improved. What I am looking for from teachers' critiques of their lesson is diagnosis and prescription. Diagnosis based on data, and prescriptions based on whatever initiative the whole coaching process was based on. I want teachers to see a way to get better by doing what we are training them to do.

THE GESTALT FOR THE THREE QUESTIONS

The over-arching rationale for the three questions is to get teachers to self-reflect and to get them talking.

Once the teacher has answered all three questions, she will have talked long enough to provide me with something about the lesson that I can glom onto. If a teacher says, 'I thought it went okay but if I were to teach it again, I might change _____.' My response is, 'You know, ___ is exactly what I wanted to discuss with you.'

Is that a lie? No. Is that *exactly* what I wanted to talk to her about? It is exactly *one* of the things I wanted to talk about. It is exactly what I wanted to talk about if it is related to the initiative that is the focus of coaching. It is important to talk about what the teacher thinks is important. Ten minutes is not a long time. Remember to adhere to the structure.

Suddenly we are engaged in a conversation about what she wants to talk about. The teacher can walk away from the meeting feeling her diagnosis, her intuition, her data, were all interpreted correctly.

THERE IS NO NEED TO EMBARRASS

When I am hired by a school to coach teachers, I want the principal to be present during all phases of the coaching cycle. In fact, before I begin working with a school the principal must agree that she, or a representative, will be present for all meetings. There are several reasons for this.

A teacher who really needs to improve will not improve because an outside person comes into their classroom and says they should do this or do that. It is up to the teacher to decide to improve. Ultimately it is up to the principal to ensure teachers are providing quality instruction.

Unfortunately, I have had to meet with teachers and their principal to discuss lessons that were disasters. I recall more than once after such a post-observation conference the principal told me something like, 'You're too nice. Why didn't you tell them how bad the lesson was? Did you think that lesson was okay? What are you getting paid to do?'

I am not sure what they wanted me to do. Of course, I thought the lesson was awful. But my job is to help teachers get better, not to berate them. The question that should be going through your mind when observing a lesson is, 'What is the one piece of feedback I could give that would make a positive impact on this teacher's instruction?'

If I blast a teacher who benefits? Most teachers who are not doing a good job are aware of that fact. It makes no sense to alienate them before we have had a chance to develop a relationship.

If a teacher needs to be reprimanded it should not be done by a visitor to their classroom who they might see two or three times. If a teacher needs to have a more intense conversation it should come from the principal, in private, at a more appropriate time.

When is an appropriate time for a principal to blast a teacher? I don't know the right time, but the wrong time is when it can be associated with you, the coach, and the coaching process in general.

My job is to help teachers get better. But that isn't my only job. My job is to also work with the principal to help teachers to get better. If a teacher is so bad that there is nothing that I can do during a 10-minute conference to help them get better … then I will need several coaching sessions with that teacher and several meetings discussing improvement plans with the principal.

There is another important reason not to blast a teacher. You should be aware that teachers talk about their interactions with a coach. If you go off on a colleague – or not even go off but are factually accurate about how badly a terrible lesson sucked – you will not only lose that teacher, but also every one of the teachers in her circle. You will lose all the trust and relationship building that you have worked so hard to create with staff.

To get back to the relationship analogy, you don't just break up with her, you break up with her entire family.

LIMIT WHAT YOU DISCUSS

During the pre-observation meeting you will have discussed goals and targets that were driven by the school's areas of focus. In the post-observation conference topics should be limited to these pre-observation objectives. You only have 10-15 minutes. You must stay focused. Beyond a 'celebration' of something from the lesson, stick to what was previously agreed to be most important.

Topics beyond those areas of focus should be acknowledged and noted for later follow-up. Not having time to complete the conversation can be a good thing. Ask for another 'date' to talk further.

#1 Limit your suggestions

Two suggestions are the maximum. Suggestions should be about the areas of focus, suggestions that will impact other parts of lessons as well.

You can't tell them everything you know. They may love what you have to say but they won't remember most of it. 'But I explained it so well.' They won't remember it. 'But I know this teacher. She will remember it.' They won't remember it.

Caution! Never believe a teacher who says, 'Tell me everything. I just want to get better.' When a teacher says this what she really means is, 'I know I am an outstanding teacher. Please tell me how wonderful I am!'

#2 Check for understanding

You never know what teachers will take away from your feedback. I always end the session with this, 'I talked a lot during these 10 minutes and made several suggestions. This is my check for understanding. What did you hear me say?'

Their responses usually need to be clarified; this is a good thing. Provide clarification on the points, check for understanding again.

#3 Have a follow up form

Keep it simple. The form I use has three questions:

- What is something you like, learned, or remembered from the coaching cycle?
- Why is this important to you?
- What additional support would you like?

The form serves several purposes. It provides individual data that can be aggregated to determine staff growth and needs. It affirms the teacher's view of what is important versus being told what is important (an important concept in adult learning theory). It provides data for possible whole staff PD topics. It also provides you with an opportunity to schedule follow-up work.

YOU CAN'T TELL THEM EVERYTHING YOU KNOW

One of the reasons you were selected as a coach is that you demonstrated excellence as a teacher. Experts seem to do so many things so effortlessly, so smoothly, that someone not familiar with teaching would miss most of the subtleties that made you a special teacher. When working with teachers, you embody the adage 'I have probably forgotten more than you know.'

It takes years to gain the knowledge that you have gleaned. Why would you think someone with less experience and expertise could understand, much less apply, all that you know in less time. Others not as experienced as you are not able to comprehend the things you know, so don't try to tell them – at least not now.

Remember when you had your own classroom, and you would begin a new unit? You would build knowledge as the unit progressed. You knew it was important not to overwhelm your students. Little by little, lesson by lesson, you brought your class along. You held back information that you knew that they would just love, but you waited until they were ready, until they had the experience to appreciate the wonder of the content. As the students approached each of their learning milestones, they produced something special to demonstrate their current level of knowledge. Until then, you knew they were not ready for more.

Is there any reason to believe the teachers you are working with are any different? Do not overwhelm them with your wisdom. Providing too much information is just as bad as not providing enough.

TALKING SO TEACHERS WILL LISTEN

One of the reasons you were selected to be a coach is that you demonstrated excellence as a teacher. Your classes consistently achieved at a level that exceeded many other classes, they behaved appropriately, your teaching experience covered multiple grade levels, and you exceeded expectations as a staff member. You should be proud of all those achievements. And although all those experiences are admirable, they are baseline achievements for a coach.

Another quality I am sure you possess is an above average ability to communicate. Although not listed in the accomplishments above, effective communication is an important, and necessary, skill for a coach to possess. The need for effective communication skills is universally addressed in every book on coaching – including this one.

Usually, the skills are broken down into various sub-categories such as listening, questioning, exhibiting empathy, developing rapport, etc.[15] It is easy to be drawn into the theoretical, research based, discussions about the topic. It is easy to become overwhelmed and forget that you already possess the ability to communicate. Is there more to learn? Yes, but don't overthink it.

Many years ago, I was working as a counselor at a middle school located in a small farming community in the Central Valley of California. The demographics of the school were very similar to those where I grew up. The population was approximately 92% Hispanic, 6% Filipino, and 2% other, which included a sprinkling of Caucasian students.

During lunchtime a 7th grade Hispanic girl approached me and asked, 'Mr. T., aren't you embarrassed to be white?'

I was thrown by the question and didn't answer. Instead, I skillfully changed the subject. I was so puzzled by the question that when I got home that night, I called my professor who had taught a class in multicultural counseling. I shared my interaction with the student. We spoke for at least 30 minutes discussing what might be the underlying reasons for

---

15   The depth of many of the discussions in some coaching books exceed what I learned earning a master's degree in counseling.

such a question. I thanked my professor, feeling a little bit more prepared for such a question in the future.

Sure enough, a couple weeks later the same 7th grade Hispanic girl asked, 'Mr. T. aren't you embarrassed to be white?'

By this time, I had completely forgotten the discussion with my professor. I had forgotten all the possible theoretical bases for such an inquiry. I responded simply with my own question, 'Why do you ask?'

In a very matter of fact manner, she pointed to the playground and said, 'Look at the white kids. They are all dirty. They are the poorest kids in the school.'

If I had done what my previously unsophisticated, ill-educated communications skills had guided me to do and simply asked a clarifying question I could have responded immediately to the student's question. I could have saved 30 minutes of my professor's and my own time as well as gaining insight into the culture of the community. The moral of this story is simple. You need to sharpen some skills, but don't overthink it.

Effective communication is one of those skills necessary in coaching. However, don't sell yourself short, your skills are already above average. Below is an organizational structure to help improve your listening, questioning, and empathy skills.

At one time or another you have probably taken a short test to determine your personality type. If you haven't taken one yet, I am sure you soon will. They are a popular staple of PD. The Myers-Briggs personality type indicator is one such test. True Colors is another popular test given to teaching staff. The Enneagram is another. There are many such tests that claim to describe your personality using one or more categories and subcategories. These categories and subcategories describe a person's needs and how they operate in the world to satisfy those needs.

Psychologists note these tests do not hold up to scientific and statistical scrutiny for either validity or reliability. Although not scientific, I have found one set of characteristics, or needs, to be useful in improving communications with teachers – and there is no need to take a test. All you need to do is pay attention to how the person communicates. These characteristics are:

- Identity: Their identity is tied to being a teacher.
- Connection: They feel best when connecting with students and colleagues.
- Competence: Their self-esteem is tied to being a very good teacher.
- Purpose: They feel they were put on earth to be a teacher.
- Power: Like Frank Sinatra, they want to do it 'my way'.
- Fun: If it's not fun find a way to make it fun.

At any given moment most people are attempting to satisfy one or more of those needs. For a teacher to believe that a coach is being effective and supporting them, the coach must make the teacher believe that she is helping the teacher satisfy her most dominant needs. A successful coach will help the teacher satisfy needs that even the teacher themselves may not consciously recognize.

But how can a coach help a teacher satisfy a dominant need when the teacher herself doesn't even know that she is trying to satisfy that need? The first step is to listen carefully to the teacher. There will only be one or two of the six needs above a teacher may be trying to satisfy in a given moment. You should be able to identify those need(s) quickly. You already have a one in six chance just by guessing. The odds are even more in your favor because often people have a primary need and a secondary need that is the driving force in the moment.

Expert tip: Most teachers mirror the students who they teach. For example, elementary teachers are more apt to have a primary need for connection just like their students. Middle school teachers are often looking to fulfill their need for fun. Whereas secondary teachers may be looking to satisfy the need for power.

These are not hard and fast rules, but they do give you a place to start as you listen.

Imagine the following scenarios.

Scenario #1

You have just observed an elementary school teacher teach a lesson. During the post-observation meeting the teacher reports that not enough students were engaged. She asks for suggestions about how to improve student engagement.

Guessing that the dominant need of the teacher is connection, you respond by suggesting that a pair share, with students taking turns who goes first, might be a strategy to consider. You explain that you have observed her colleagues using the pair share strategy so she would fit right in with other teachers at the school.

Scenario #2

You have just observed a middle school teacher teach a lesson. During the post-observation meeting she reports not enough students were engaged. She asks for suggestions about how to improve student engagement.

Guessing that the dominant need of the teacher is fun, you may respond by saying that a pair share, with students taking turns who goes first, might be a strategy to consider. You explain that it is more fun for students to share an answer with a friend prior to being called on. You tell her other teachers have fun with the students by having silly ways to decide which partners go first. For example, 'The partner with a birthday closest to Halloween goes first.'

Scenario #3

You have just observed a high school teacher teach a lesson. During the post-observation meeting the teacher reports not enough students were engaged. She asks for suggestions about how to improve student engagement.

Guessing that the dominant need of the teacher is to satisfy the need for power, you respond by saying that some type of pair share might be a strategy to consider. You continue by explaining to the teacher, 'There is no strict or exact way that a pair share needs to be designed. If you think it is something you may want to try, feel free to customize it to make it work for you.'

Each scenario has the same classroom issue, the same suggestions for improvement, but the message is delivered in a slightly different manner honoring each teacher's individual needs.

Of course, not all elementary teachers share the primary need for love and belonging. Not all middle school teachers have the primary need for fun. And not all high school teachers have the primary need for power. These are just a place to start listening from.

If you gave feedback as suggested above to the elementary teacher and she replies, 'I don't care what my colleagues are doing. I want my students to have fun and I want to have fun.' You now know the teacher's primary need. And it only took you two tries!

There is a hybrid-need seeking teacher of whom you should be aware. This teacher can be found at all grade levels, and if not communicated with properly can cause lasting issues. The teacher's primary need is a hybrid fusion of competence and power. This teacher believes she is always the smartest person in the room.

The only way to earn this teacher's respect is to show them how smart you are. Paradoxically, all you need to do is let her know you recognize how smart she is. She will think, 'Only a smart person would recognize my superior intellect.'

Teachers will feel that you really understand them … because you do. If you are helping to satisfy an individual's primary need, they are more likely to feel you understand them. If they feel you understand them, then you are better at understanding their problems. This in turn makes them more likely to be open to listening to suggestions. This dynamic is unconscious, but still powerful.

POWER PHRASES

Below are a few phrases I have found to be helpful during post-observation meetings.

- When a teacher talks too much: 'You work too hard!'
- When a teacher is reluctant to believe there may be a more effective way to do something. 'Be a scientist. Think of this strategy as an experiment.'

- When a teacher never checks students understanding during the lesson: 'I know you know the information. I don't know if all your students know it.'
- When a teacher only calls on the few same students to answer questions: 'Which students need to know this information?'

LAST WORDS

Many post-observation meetings conclude with the teacher saying, 'That's it? That wasn't bad at all. In fact, I enjoyed this; I learned a lot.'

Without a moment's hesitation, I respond, 'Tell your friends.' They smile. Then I add, 'I am serious as a heart attack. Let your friends know you thought it was worth the time and effort.'

FREQUENTLY ASKED QUESTIONS

Question: What if the lesson was a disaster?

Answer: If the lesson was a disaster, do not ask the teacher how they think the lesson went. What if they say they thought it was fine? Then you have nowhere to go.

In over 97% of the cases in which a lesson did not go well, the coach does not have to start the conversation. The teacher will suggest how poorly the lesson went. If the teacher says it was bad, ask them to identify some specific thing they thought went badly.

If the teacher does not offer that the lesson was bad, start with an observational question and a compliment that is objectively true, possibly a non-compliment compliment. 'Does Johnny always behave like that? You appeared to have a lot of experience dealing with that behavior.'

Question: Should I use checklists during the post-observation meeting?

Answer: Checklists can create more problems than they solve. Checklists create artificial benchmarks that can allow teachers to miss the forest for the trees. An ineffective teacher may hit every mark on a checklist and still be ineffective. Effective teachers may lose confidence in a coach because they know that quality instruction is more than checking boxes.

A teacher who is less than effective, could hit 10 of the 15 items on the list and wrongly believe their instruction was good. Their misguided goal becomes to get those last five items checked off even if the last five items do not significantly impact her instruction. Even if the true area that needs to be improved is an item that was already checked off. In this case, the checklist becomes a hinderance to the post-observation reflection and feedback session and will have little real impact on the teacher's instruction.

A more effective teacher could look at a checklist and decide that increasing the effectiveness of a single component on the list would have the most impact on her instruction. For this teacher, the checklist also becomes a hinderance to the post-observation reflection and feedback session and has little real impact on her instruction.

Another issue with using checklists is that teachers talk to each other. Teachers wonder why their colleagues had more items crossed off the checklist than they did. They become upset with the coach. The coaching relationship is negatively impacted. Trust in the coach is lost.

Checklists are about compliance. Coaching is about quality.

Question: What if the teacher does not bring up any of the items I had noted during the observation as things that need to be discussed?

Answer: Do what politicians do. Politicians begin to answer a question that has been asked, but then pivot quickly to discuss something different. Be sure to touch on the teacher's issue before you pivot. Conclude your answer with, 'I am not sure I answered your question.' Usually, the teacher will be good with your response.

Question: I have been told I should not directly answer a teacher's questions. Supposedly I should respond to questions with phrases such as, 'What do you think?'

Answer: Imagine going into a building supply store and asking a store employee for advice on the proper type of lumber to use for the fence you are building. How you would feel if the employee's response was, 'What do you think would work best?'

Your reaction would probably be something like, 'If I knew what the best was, I wouldn't be asking you!'

It is the same with teachers and coaches. If a teacher asks a direct question such as, 'How is cold calling different from just calling on random students?' Then the teacher is looking to their coach as an expert, someone with answers. In your capacity as an expert, teachers will come to you with specific questions and problems for which they are hoping to find both help and answers.

I have seen suggestions in training literature that an acceptable response to such a question would be, 'That's a good question. I have an article in my office about that very thing. I'll get you a copy.'

A direct question deserves a direct answer. The coach should give a clear cogent response. If you don't know the answer, admit it readily and then go find the answer. Once the coach and teacher are satisfied that they have a common understanding of the differences between cold calling and calling on random students, *then* the coach can ask a reflective question such as, 'How different is this description of cold calling to how you currently call on students?'

Your job as a coach is to help the teacher be more effective, not to serve as a curator of information that you could have shared orally in 30 seconds.

First answer the question as an expert, this enhances your status as a resource; then have the teacher reflect on the impact on their practice.

PART FOUR

MISCELLANEOUS TIPS AND GETTING STARTED

TIPS

Big ideas:

- Principals are not coaches.
- Concierge coach.
- Don't do demonstration lessons.
- Demonstrating a tool.
- Don't send novices to watch lessons alone.
- Having to be right.
- Karma.
- Never ask a colleague to practice on them.
- What to do when a teacher cries.

OVERVIEW

This part of the book contains tips and bits of advice that I have learned over the years. Some of it I learned, as the saying goes, the hard way. While some of my tips are the exact opposite of what you may find in other coaching books, I stand by them.

PRINCIPALS ARE NOT COACHES

Principals, as much as you may want to coach your teachers, you cannot. The reason has nothing to do with your knowledge or skills. In fact, it has nothing to do with you at all. The reason you cannot be a coach is the power differential inherent between a principal and a teacher. The principal has the responsibility to evaluate, discipline, and reprimand and the teacher is subject to being evaluated, disciplined, and reprimanded. However, even though you cannot coach, there is plenty in this book to help you sharpen your skills as you work with teachers to hopefully help them to be more effective.

The most frequent argument I hear from principals who want to coach is, 'I have a great relationship with my staff.' That may be true, but the administrator is not the individual in the relationship who gets to judge the type of relationship they have. It is the teacher who is being coached who decides.

The situation is analogous to a student reporting to a school official that she is being the victim of harassment or bullying. The adult in charge calls in those students who have been accused of bullying behavior. The accused students state they weren't bullying the student, they were just joking. The person who reported the bullying didn't think, or feel, they were joking.

We all know that the person who gets to judge whether something makes them uncomfortable is the person with less power or status. It is clear where the power lies between the principal and teacher. Work with the coach to help teachers get better. Trust the coach to do her job. You do your job.

CONCIERGE COACH

I love staying in hotels that have a concierge. You want a recommendation for an Italian restaurant? Ask the concierge. Need tickets to an amusement park? Ask the concierge.

There are times when a concierge may make a trip to the liquor store to personally make a special purchase for you. Occasionally they personally make deliveries to your room fulfilling exotic requests. However, the strength of an outstanding concierge is their vast network of independent contractors.

A concierge is not judged by who physically performs the requested task, but rather by its performance and the quality of the results. To be effective, the concierge knows how to get things done, and she knows her limitations. Similarly, an instructional coach does not need to personally perform all tasks necessary to help a teacher get better. The coach can provide additional help by developing a network of quality connections.

As the instructional coach, you are part of a system to support teachers.

You do not need to be an expert on every aspect of the curriculum, assessment, and/or mental health. Like the concierge, you should develop a network of skilled people each of whom have a unique skillset and whose job it is to support teachers; think specialists in content areas, edtech, special education, etc.

As you develop more trusting relationships with teachers, they may share non-work related, personal issues. You are not a counselor. The extent to which you provide support in such a situation is limited to what a friend might provide. You are not a counselor, but make sure a counselor or other helping professional is part of your network.

Before you refer teachers to work with other specialists in your district, take time to become familiar with that specialist and their work. Be sure they share your values. The referral becomes a reflection on you. It is very easy for someone to undo all the work you have done with a teacher.

Being known to teachers as the person in the district to go to when they need assistance is a desirable position to hold. Wise is the person who knows they do not know; wiser still is the coach who knows someone who *does* know.

DON'T DO DEMONSTRATION LESSONS

Many other books and resources advise coaches to create and distribute a menu of services to entice teachers into meeting with them. Coaches are strongly encouraged to list demonstration lessons, or demos, on their menu of services. What follows is the good, the bad, and the ugly of demonstration lessons (spoiler alert: the good is not good either.)

THE GOOD

The primary purpose of a demo is to be invited into classrooms of teachers who don't want to participate in coaching. Demo lessons are sold to coaches as a good initial activity that introduces teachers to the knowledge and talents of the coach. Demo lessons are considered a low-risk activity for coaches because there is no face-to-face interaction with the teacher. How to initiate and conduct face-to-face interactions with teachers is the number one question that is asked by new coaches. Demo lessons are considered a low-risk activity for teachers because they have zero responsibility during the lesson and therefore have zero exposure to the coach's scrutiny.

There are coaches who strongly disagree with my admonition, 'Don't do demonstration lessons.' However, in my experience – even in the best of circumstances – no positive changes will occur in the host teacher's instructional practices from demo lessons. Those coaches, arguing for doing demos have told me, 'I love doing demos! The teachers love to see me being successful with their students.' I don't doubt that. Most teachers enjoy seeing their kids being successful. They have also told me, 'The kids loved it. Students love having guest teachers.' (As an aside, students also love attending assemblies.) As a coup de grace, coaches report that teachers have told them, 'Come back anytime!' All those statements may be true and yet none of them address the efficacy of demonstration lessons at helping teachers improve.

The purpose of coaching is to help teachers improve instructional practices. Doing a demonstration lesson does not help a teacher get better. It is a waste of time for the coach and the teacher. Let me prove that quickly.

Imagine you are teaching a child to ride a bike. There are several methods to teach a child, but one that is never used is this: You get on the bike, and you tell the child, 'Watch me ride your bike.' You ride the bike a few yards, turn around, and return to the child. You then say, 'Riding a bike is not as easy as it looks. Watch me ride again.' You ride the bike a few more yards, turn around, and return to the child. Finally, you say, 'Let me demonstrate one more time. Then I will leave and let you practice on your own.'

How many times would you need to demonstrate before the child is able to ride a bike themselves? A trick question, right? No one teaches a child to ride a bike by having them watch a demonstration. Children learn to ride by getting on the bike and riding while being supported.

A teacher does not learn a new strategy by watching a coach. A teacher learns by using the new strategy with support from the coach. An effective coach supports teachers by providing just-in-time feedback as the teacher attempts new strategies. Not by telling the teacher, 'Watch me.'

Even positive affective outcomes, such as those described by advocates of demonstration lessons above, do not always result. The bottom line is that, even in the best-case scenario, demonstration lessons will not result in improved teacher effectiveness.

THE BAD

It is possible that your demo does not go as well as planned. Even the most experienced and effective teachers have lessons that do not come off as planned. When you are teaching a demo lesson that is intended to be an exemplar, in a new classroom, with students unknown to you, the chances of something happening to derail the lesson increases.

Below is a list of possible issues:

- Behavior issues with students who the coach does not know.

Even coaches who were experts managing their own classroom can encounter unexpected behaviors that can sabotage a lesson.

- No prior knowledge of students.

Frequently lessons require or build on prior knowledge or skills. It is not unusual for a host teacher to over report their students' knowledge or skills to the coach.

- Personality or style mismatch

The coach's style is so different to the teacher's that the teacher cannot see herself using the strategy.

I once worked with a young coach who had enjoyed great success as a teacher. This coach had been a cheerleader in high school. When she did demo lessons, she was very high energy using strategies that she had used as a teacher. The coach told me she drew on her cheerleading experience while teaching by leading the students in an original 'rap' she had created for each lesson to help students remember the content presented. All her demonstration lessons were high energy and included a rap. Unfortunately, the understandable response from many teachers was, 'I am not doing a rap.' Teachers also wondered, 'Do they think I am so bad that I need someone to demonstrate how to teach?'

THE UGLY

Over the years I have witnessed several downsides for a coach doing a demo lesson, and not many upsides for the teacher who is observing. Let's talk about those downsides.

What if the teacher does not believe in the innovation being presented by the coach and has simply asked them into their classroom to 'check the box' of agreeing to host a demo lesson? The teacher has then fulfilled their obligation to meet with the coach, has watched a lesson, and can now honestly say she has seen the innovation and it was not for her. This leaves the coach with nowhere to go.

What if the teacher has no intention of adopting the innovation being presented and hopes the coach's demonstration lesson fails? Is it likely a teacher with this attitude will be so impressed by the demo lesson that they will invite the coach into their classroom afterwards?

What if the teacher agrees to have the coach do a demonstration lesson, but then simply sits at her desk grading papers, answering emails, or performing some other task that takes her attention from the coach and the lesson they are teaching. I have even seen teachers leave the classroom during a demo lesson.

This behavior might seem rude but is not hard to understand if you take the perspective of the teacher who believes she is doing the coach a favor by allowing her to 'practice' on her class.

What is it that you are trying to accomplish by teaching a lesson to a host teacher's class? Are you trying to prove that you can teach content better than the regular teacher? Are you indirectly giving the message to the teacher that if she were better more of her students would be achieving more? Are you trying to prove that you are a good teacher?

Assume your principal has told all teachers they would be meeting with you. What is the profile of the teacher who volunteers to welcome you into her classroom to teach a demo lesson? It is most likely a teacher who is already open to meeting with you in your role as a coach. If so, then what have you gained? Are you looking for a teacher to create a good buzz about how good your lesson was?

Skip the demo; schedule a coaching cycle.

DEMONSTRATING A TOOL

Imagine you are learning to play guitar and you discover there is an on-line app that will help you tune your guitar. You already know how to tune a guitar, you have used other methods, but you are intrigued by this new app so you meet a friend who has offered to demonstrate it.

Your friend begins to tell you about the importance of keeping your guitar tuned. He explains how easily it can get out of tune. How certain songs put strings under more stress and therefore may tend to make the guitar lose its tuning more quickly. He explains how there are different ways to tune your guitar. He goes on and on.

Finally, you tell him, 'Just show me how to use this app.'

It is very common for districts to have instructional coaches for each discipline and program area such as math, ELD, ELA, science, STEM, STEAM, and others. In addition to these discipline area coaches, edtech coaches are also very common.

Edtech coaches are tasked with staying up to date on the plethora of education 'innovations' presented on new and various platforms that are continuously being introduced. Each new platform seems to do what the previous 'latest' platform did except that this one is easier to use, or it has a new feature that a competitor platform lacks, or something to make it unique in the marketplace. It is up to the edtech coaches to keep up to date and sample all that is new, so that the teachers do not have to. In fact, all content area coaches have the same responsibility of staying up to date and sharing the latest innovations in their respective fields with staff.

Once a new platform passes muster, then the coach is responsible for introducing this innovation and training staff. This can be done in a variety of ways. It might be introduced through some media that has been produced by the edtech coach and made available to the staff. Maybe it will be introduced to the entire staff as part of a regularly scheduled meeting or PD. There are a number of other ways. However, this new platform should not be introduced by teaching an entire lesson with it in a single classroom for an individual teacher.

As stated earlier do not to do demonstration lessons. It is not necessary for a classroom teacher to lose an entire class period when you only need to demonstrate a tweak (especially if it is only a slight variation to current practice that needs to be learned and practiced by the teacher).

Demonstrate the technique, tweak, or variation.

Observe the teacher practicing the variation. Provide feedback to the teacher. In most cases, since the teacher is in the middle of a lesson, a 'thumbs up' will suffice.

DON'T SEND NOVICES TO WATCH LESSONS ALONE

A person does not need to be a literary scholar to enjoy a great novel. 'What did I think of the themes? I guess I didn't notice. What did I think of the symbolism? I guess I didn't notice. I really liked the ending. It was a really good story.'

Watching an expert teacher in the classroom is a lot like reading a great novel. A person who knows little of the technical aspects and subtleties of running a classroom may leave an observation thinking the teacher is good, but not know why.

A novice teacher may observe a teacher whose students follow routines for every aspect of student movement from entering the room, to getting materials, to handing in work, etc. The novice, without someone to mediate the experience, may leave an observation thinking, 'The students were so well behaved. I liked the way the teacher used the clothes pins to record student behavior levels. I am going to try that.'

The novice noticed the clothes pins, but what she did not see was weeks of teaching, practicing, training, providing feedback … and more teaching, practicing, training, and providing feedback.

If you are recommending that a novice teacher observe an element of instruction that they would benefit from, be there with her. Sit next to her. Describe what is happening and what had to happen in order to make that work.

HAVING TO BE RIGHT

You were selected to be a coach because someone believed you have the skills and knowledge to do the job. You possess a certain level of expertise. Do you know what that *doesn't* mean? It doesn't mean that every helpful hint you give will be accepted. It doesn't mean that every suggestion you give a teacher will be taken positively. It doesn't even mean that you will be believed. Most importantly, it does not mean you will always be right.

I have been coaching teachers for nearly 20 years. Not to toot my own horn, but there have been many teachers who have improved greatly because of my coaching. There have been educators whose careers have been saved because of what they learned from me. There have been teachers whose entire work personalities changed from being negative and blaming everything possible for their students' lack of success to being a role model of positivity for other teachers.

With that being said, *I have never convinced a teacher to try anything!* Every teacher who has ever tried to implement a single suggestion I put forward did so because they decided to try it, not because I convinced them of my point of view.

What is the subtext when you are trying to convince a teacher to do something different? What a teacher hears is, 'Are you telling me I don't know how to teach? Are you telling me I have been doing this wrong for all these years?'

If that is the message a teacher is hearing (and please believe me, that is the message many teachers will be hearing), do you think she cares about the research you are quoting? Do you think she appreciates how cleverly you used her argument against her? Do you think she is going to change because everyone else in her grade-level is successful with the strategy you are suggesting? Not only does she not care, but she has also stopped listening to you.

Do you know what is worse than her not listening to you? It is you not listening to her. All the time you are trying to convince her to do something, she does not feel that you are listening to her.

Strategies that work:

1. Tell the teacher to think about your suggestion like an experiment. 'Try it and see how it works. If the students don't respond positively then stop doing it.' (Notice I put the onus on the student data and not on whether she likes it.)

2. Use a network of fans and other teachers with whom you have worked and helped to generate good buzz. At the end of any coaching encounter if the teacher says something like, 'This was really good', or 'I learned a lot', then I always say, 'Tell your friends!' They laugh as if I am joking, but I let them know I am as serious as a heart attack.

3. Tell the teacher, 'I have an idea. If you like my idea smile and say, "I like that." If you don't like the idea, just smile.'

4. Maybe this is a teacher who should be working with an administrator; not to be coached, but possibly to be counseled out of the profession.

You can't win them all. You want to be a Hall of Fame baseball player? Successfully get a hit one out three times you are at bat (I know that cliche has been used to death, but it is the truth). Your success rate with teachers you coach should be much higher than 30%, but you will not be successful with them all. In most districts there is more than one coach. Maybe the teacher will respond better to someone else.

KARMA

There is an apocryphal story that I heard told about Gandhi which demonstrates how a coach must think about their job.

A woman gets an appointment for herself and her son to meet with Mahatma Gandhi. The Mahatma asks what he can do for her. The mother replies, 'I need help with my son. He eats too much sugar. I have tried everything to get him to eat less sugar. I was hoping that you might talk to him.'

Gandhi replies to the woman, 'Come back in two weeks.'

Two weeks later the mother and son return to meet with the Mahatma. Gandhi looks at the young man and says, 'Stop eating sugar.'

The mother quizzically, angrily, asks, 'That's it? Why didn't you tell him that two weeks ago?'

Gandhi replies, 'Because two weeks ago I was eating sugar.'

Regardless of your belief systems here are some aphorisms for you to consider now that you are a coach:

- What goes around comes around.
- If you are going to talk the talk you need to walk the walk.
- Karma can be a cruel teacher.

One of your many responsibilities as a coach will be to do presentations to your staff. The presentations may be very short bits of information such as updates to schedules, announcing or reporting on events, etc. You may also be called upon to make longer presentations.

I recommend that you take an inventory of how *you* behave in similar circumstances. During a staff meeting, do you give the speaker your full attention? Or are you checking email, texting, or chatting with a colleague? During a training session do you grade papers? Do you continually tell everyone at your table why the presenter is wrong? Is boring? Has typos in their materials, etc. If you resemble these remarks, how will you respond to an audience that does the same thing to you?

When you make commitments to colleagues to have your part of a project done, do you always keep those commitments? Are your contributions to problem solving and brainstorming positive or snarky? When you say you will be somewhere are you on time? When you have an issue with someone do you have a direct conversation with that person, or do you gossip behind their back?

It is time to stop eating sugar and model the behaviors you expect from the teachers you will be coaching.

NEVER ASK A COLLEAGUE TO PRACTICE ON THEM

I often look at a situation and ask myself, 'What are all the things that could go wrong?' This is not because I am a pessimist, it is because I want to avoid or mitigate as many worst-case scenarios as possible before they occur.

Many resources suggest that coaches ask colleagues to allow them to practice coaching techniques on them. This suggestion is usually offered because many coaches find themselves in a situation where they have no one to coach, and no one is volunteering. (This is in schools where the principal has not told all teachers they will be meeting with the coach.)

The suggestion to ask friends to allow you to 'practice' coaching on them makes sense in that it allows you to coach, but there are several possible unintended negative consequences. Let's examine a few of these from the point of view of other staff through a few scenarios.

Scenario #1

You ask a friend to allow you to 'practice' coach her.

This may have the unintended consequence that your colleague is upset that they are being asked to help train the coach without being compensated.

If you have been selected as a coach it is likely that you are an experienced teacher who is not at the bottom of the salary schedule. It is also possible you may have received a small stipend or some other type of small salary bump. When you ask a colleague, a friend, who is less senior than you to allow you to practice on them, their perception may be that you are asking someone who makes less money to train you.

Scenario #2

You are working with your colleague/friend, when you are interrupted by another teacher who sees the two of you. The interrupting teacher apologizes and begins to close the door when your friend says, 'Oh that's okay. She was just practicing on me.' The other teacher leaves.

Would it be unreasonable for a teacher who is reluctant to be coached to object, 'I have been teaching for 10 years and I am going to be coached by someone who is still practicing?'

Teachers talk informally all the time in the staff lounge, in the hallway, and anywhere else in the school. The interrupting teacher shares with her friends that the coach was 'practicing', and it quickly gets around that the new coach, with whom every teacher is being told to meet, doesn't really have the expertise or skills so she is practicing on her friends.

Scenario #3

You are working with your colleague, friend, and she agrees with everything. There is no real, authentic, give and take.

During the entire coaching session your friend treats you, and the entire practice coaching session, in a very condescending manner. She may not actually say this, but her entire demeanor says, 'How cute that you are practicing being a coach.'

Am I exaggerating? As I said above, I always try to imagine the worst possible case. It may not happen like this, but then again it may. Is there an alternative to asking people to practice with you? Remember the reason you were asking friends to practice on is because you did not have enough teachers to coach 'for real'.

Here are some suggestions for alternatives to asking colleagues to practice on them if you are coaching in school where the principal has not told everyone to meet with the coach.

ALTERNATIVE SUGGESTIONS

Instead of asking a friend to allow you to 'practice', reframe the request. Don't put down your experience, elevate your colleague by saying, 'Angela, as you know I am supposed to be working with every teacher this year, but there are some teachers who are reluctant to work with me. You are one of the most respected teachers on the staff. You have a lot of influence. If you would agree to work with me, it would go a long way to influencing other staff members to work with me. Would you be open to being one of the first teachers to work with me?'

A word of caution on this one: You better be good. You better be sure your friend recognizes a benefit from working with you.

Chances are you are not the first coach who has worked at the school site. Ask your friend about their experience with the prior coach? Did they participate in coaching? If not, why not? Demonstrate to the colleague you are different. You are not there to show how smart you are. You want to learn from everyone.

WHAT TO DO WHEN A TEACHER CRIES

Although a teacher crying during a coaching cycle is rare, it does occur more frequently than you might think. Usually when a teacher cries it has little to do with you and what you are doing. Tears can occur at any time during a coaching cycle. However, the timing is significant and *when* a teacher cries (during a coaching cycle, pre-observation, observation, or post-observation) will help you determine how you will address it.

CRYING DURING THE PRE-OBSERVATION MEETING

Crying during the pre-observation is the rarest of the rare. There are some teachers who are so emotionally fragile that having to go through a teaching cycle becomes the straw that breaks the camel's back. Some possible reasons for stressors that have nothing to do with you or what you are doing include:

- Many teachers are working parents, sometime single parents, who have many responsibilities and are under tremendous pressure outside of the classroom.
- Coaching is not perceived as helpful and is seen as just another thing, another pressure.
- They are not confident in their teaching; they feel they will be exposed.
- They do not belong in teaching.

How to respond: Ask if they need a little break? Provide some tissue. Tell them to feel free to get a little water. The assumption with all these actions is that the planning will continue. Crying does not absolve them of the responsibility to meet with you.

Obviously, this meeting will not be as productive as you would like, but it is what it is.

If the teacher is struggling professionally, then their lack of success can make every day more miserable than the last. You must have the belief that the lives of the teachers you coach will improve because they meet with you.

CRYING DURING THE OBSERVATION

It is also rare for teachers to cry during an observation. Teachers who cry during observations will fall into one of two categories:

- New teachers who want to prove themselves.
- Experienced teachers whose motivating forces are identity as a teacher and competence.

For both categories of teacher, they might cry in a lesson when something unexpected happens, and the teacher cannot figure out how to get things back on track.

This usually occurs when the teacher is trying some new technique or strategy. Because the strategy is new, the teacher's usual responses to the situation are not available to her. These teachers have so much confidence in their teaching ability that encountering a situation from which they cannot recover throws them into a flight or fight response.

This is exactly the situation I discussed with the teacher during the pre-observation. 'You will be trying some things that are new to you. If you are in the middle of the lesson and you have a question, just look at me and ask. We will have a conversation about how to proceed.' Unfortunately, the type of teacher who may cry during the lesson is also the type who is also hesitant to ask for help.

During the pre-observation, in addition to telling the teacher that she could ask for help, you also told her you would raise your hand to ask a cuing question. A cuing question suggests a course of action that would solve the problem or at least get them back on track. By the time a teacher begins to cry, she will do everything she can to avoid eye contact with you so the raising your hand strategy is rendered mute.

At this point the lesson is effectively over, and most teachers will officially end it. I observed one teacher who became so upset and flustered that she actually left the room in the middle of the lesson. At this point there is nothing for you to do except to leave. Make as graceful an exit as you can. You will have an opportunity to chat with the teacher during the post-observation – although teachers in the categories listed above can become so embarrassed that they will avoid meeting with you. That is okay. You are playing the long game.

DURING POST-OBSERVATION MEETING

Teachers who cry during the post-observation are usually disappointed in themselves. They put pressure on themselves to be perfect. Their expectations for the lesson were high, but they missed the mark.

When a teacher is crying because she is disappointed in herself it is because her identity is tied to being a good teacher. She is not going to hear any of the brilliant insightful suggestions you have for her. Your goal at this point is to end the meeting on a positive note and get back to her later when she has calmed somewhat.

When I encounter this this type of situation, I try to bring some reality into the situation. I ask the teacher, 'Have you ever taught a lesson that was so good that every one of your students was successful? Have you ever taught a lesson that didn't go so well? You are not a good teacher one day and a bad teacher the next day. It is the lesson. Remember that.'

You still need to talk about the lesson, but not now. Do not even try to set a time to talk about it. Check in the next day when things are calmer. You are playing the long game.

GETTING STARTED

Big ideas:

- What else do you need to know (coaching axioms)?
- Mission creep.
- Go get 'em.

WHAT ELSE DO YOU NEED TO KNOW?

Here are a few coaching axioms that can save you a lot of time and heartache.

IT IS NEVER A GOOD TIME TO OBSERVE OR MEET WITH TEACHERS FOR COACHING CYCLES

You can't meet with teachers at the beginning of the year because:

- Classes are still being leveled/or there are schedule changes.
- We are still establishing routines.
- We are still doing assessments.
- Student rotations.
- Etc.

You can't meet next week because:

- We have a test.
- We are reviewing for a test.
- It is our library time.
- We are doing a project.
- We are doing presentations.
- It is the day before vacation.
- It is the day before the day before vacation, etc.

It will never be a 'good time' for a coaching cycle. Just schedule it and do it.

YOU WILL NOT CLICK WITH EVERYONE.

No matter how skilled you are, how much you know, or how much experience you have, there will always be a teacher with whom you just do not click. It is possible that you remind them of their ex. They think you are too old, too young, or something else that you cannot control. At one time I made it my mission to win those teachers over. No more.

It isn't so much that there are more technical things to learn, it is that you are working with people who will always provide you with unique circumstances. The master knows when enough is enough and has an alternate plan for that teacher.

Maybe the plan includes the teacher working with another coach in the district. The more likely scenario is that such a teacher should not be working you with but instead being counseled by an administrator.

BUSY IS NOT THE SAME AS EFFECTIVE.

For most of you this is your first job outside the classroom. You are no longer tied to a bell schedule. You have the freedom to create your own schedule. No one will be looking over your shoulder telling you what you need to do or when you need to do it. How you spend your day will be up to you.

There are many things you need to accomplish. There are many things you need to learn. There are many items that need to be calendared. There are numerous meetings to fit into your schedule from grade-level meetings, department meetings, meetings with your site administrator, to meetings with other coaches in your district, etc. There will be additional off-site training and conferences to improve your skills and knowledge that you will want to attend. You will need time to prepare PD for your staff. And don't forget those emergencies you will be asked to help with.

Other resources offer suggestions on how to promote yourself and your services. These suggestions are offered because the principal has not told all the teachers they will meet with the coach. The suggestions are meant to make you more attractive to teachers in hopes they will volunteer to work with you.

Suggestions include developing a menu of services, developing interest surveys for teachers to help determine PD topics you might present. And don't forget to develop a digital calendar that allows teachers to sign-up for coaching and furnishing your office to make it an inviting and comfortable environment for teachers.

There is one major activity that was not listed in either of the two paragraphs above: coaching cycles. You can justify to yourself that all of these activities are important. All these activities can keep you busy for a long time. Most can be performed without ever meeting face-to-face, one-on-one, with a teacher. The paradox is that meeting one-on-one with teachers in a coaching cycle is the quickest way to develop a relationship with teachers. Meeting one-on-one with teachers is the most effective and efficient manner of impacting instruction.

MISSION CREEP

All coaches will find themselves being asked to help or fill in whenever there is an emergency. At first it may seem a genuine emergency such as when a teacher is suddenly called away and someone needs to cover the class. Because you are a team player, you are glad to help. Or there is a long-term absence and someone needs to write lesson plans for a sub. That seems like an emergency – and you are glad to help. The person who coordinated testing in the past is no longer interested in performing those duties. Is that an emergency? You are glad to help.

It is very easy for the coach to slip into the role of the 'go to' person to fill in these miscellaneous tasks. You are obviously talented. It makes sense that you are the person to go to in these situations *if* you have not already filled your schedule with coaching teachers.

Many teachers leave their classrooms to become coaches because they see coaching as a career step into administration. You are anxious to make a good impression as a team player, so you don't want to say no when someone needs help. Being a team player, being the person who has had a variety of experiences, will help your next career move.

That might be the case, but it is a two-edged sword. By being so available to learn your next job, you neglect your current job – coaching. When looking to hire for the next position, will the people evaluating you be impressed with all your experience, or will they think less of you for not being successful as an instructional coach?

An effective coach can greatly impact a school. If you are doing all the things a coach should be doing (i.e. coaching cycles with all teachers), then you won't have time for other duties.

GO GET 'EM

Everyone has plans until they get hit for the first time.

Mike Tyson, 1987.

When Mike Tyson was asked by a reporter if he was worried about his opponent Tyrell Bigg's plans to beat him, he replied with this zinger. Like many famous quotes the wording has evolved over time into the even more memorable, 'Everyone has a plan 'till they get hit in the mouth'.

When I first began coaching teachers, I got hit in the mouth a lot. Strategies I had learned from other resources were simply not complete. When I realized I was becoming more interested in protecting myself, my self-esteem, my ego, my professional image, and my job, than I was helping teachers, I knew I needed a new reality-based model for coaching. That was when I changed my coaching martial art metaphor from boxing to aikido.

In aikido you use the opponent's own momentum to pull and push them where they already want to go. Like all professionals, teachers want to improve. Improvement is where their momentum wants to take them. Improvement is where I want to gently push and pull them.

This book started by describing the fear many coaches feel of meeting with teachers. It is only by meeting with teachers – risking getting hit in the mouth – that you get close enough to use their momentum, to help them get to where they want to go.

What coaches discover when they engage teachers is that the process is very rarely as bad as they imagined. Mark Twain is quoted as saying, 'I have known many sorrows, most of which never happened'.[16]

---

16   In a 1923 article in *The Singapore Free Press*. Twain had however died in 1910. See quoteinvestigator.com.

he techniques, tips, and strategies I've described reflect the highest espect for teachers and the teaching profession. These techniques, tips and strategies give you a place to 'grab on', to pull and push the teachers to guide them to where they already want to go.

Do not let fear of what might happen prevent you from getting started with meeting and coaching teachers. Moving forward, doing the work, risking a punch in the mouth will illuminate where the real obstacles are in helping teachers become all they want to be.

And by the way the chords for *Louie Louie* are C, F, and G.